You Can Spell

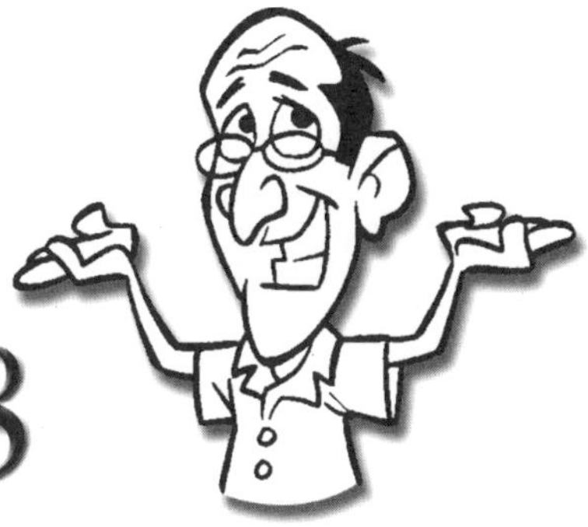

Books 5–8
Teacher's Guide

Peter De Ath

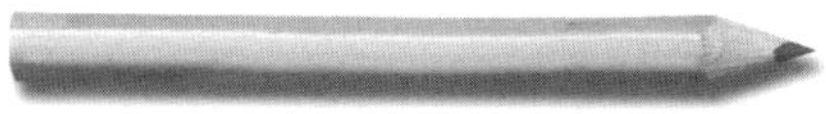

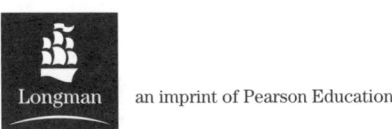

Your comments on this book are welcome at
feedback@pearsoned.co.nz

Pearson Education New Zealand Limited
46 Hillside Road, Auckland 10,
New Zealand

Associated companies throughout the world

© Pearson Education New Zealand Limited
1993, 1997, 2001

Previously published separately as *You Can Spell Teachers Guide* and *You Can Spell Blackline Master Kit* by Longman Paul 1993
Second edition published by Addison Wesley Longman New Zealand Limited 1997
Reprinted (twice) 1999
This edition published by Pearson Education
New Zealand Limited 2001

ISBN 0 582 54357 6

All rights reserved. No part of this publication may be reproduced, stored in a retrieval system, or transmitted, in any form or by any means, electronic, mechanical, photocopying, recording, or otherwise, without the prior permission of the publisher.

Produced by Pearson Education New Zealand Limited
Printed in Malaysia
Typeset in Palatino

We use **paper from sustainable forestry**

Contents

Preface to the third edition	iv
Introduction	1
Research findings	1
The spelling lists	2
The Mastery Sets	2
Working with the lists	3
Determining a starting set for each child	3
Routines	3
Activities	4
Reviews, Tough Ones and errors from previous levels	4
Supplementary learning words	4
Spelling and written expression	4
Dictation	4
Technology	5
Assessment and progress	5
About the Blackline Masters section	5
Level selection tests	7
Mastery Set 5	7
Mastery Set 6	8
Mastery Set 7	8
Mastery Set 8	9
Test Lists	10
Mastery Set 5	10
Mastery Set 6	12
Mastery Set 7	15
Mastery Set 8	18
Answers to activities in pupils' books	22
Mastery Set 5	22
Mastery Set 6	26
Mastery Set 7	30
Mastery Set 8	34
Blackline Masters	39
1 Letters to parents	39
2 Training kit	42
3 Classroom aids	44
4 Progress graphs (score sheets)	51
5 Diplomas	53
6 School records	57
7 Dictation exercises	61

Preface to the third edition

Since *You Can Spell* was first developed, users have suggested numerous modifications to improve its practical application in classrooms.

For this edition, the Teacher's Guide is produced in two separate books, one dedicated to the revised first four Mastery Sets and the associated pupils' books, and this one for use with the higher-level Mastery Sets. The revisions have even more relevance for learning to spell, and as language grows and changes, the time was right to update the word lists to incorporate newer and more frequently used words while removing those that, in only a decade, have become virtually obsolete.

In the second edition I drew attention to changes in the testing procedures. Rather than being preoccupied with testing spelling words, teachers need to devote time to ensuring that the pupils have a set of models each week that will ensure that they never learn wrong spellings. The emphasis is the same in this edition. As children record the words that they are to learn, the teacher must have a checking system built into the weekly routine.

The focus of the *You Can Spell* programme is – and has been, ever since the first edition – on the achievement of learning and mastering of spellings, not just in the short term but for all time. Both the Teacher's Guide and the new pupils' books repeatedly remind teachers and pupils of the importance of mastery learning through regular reviews of earlier lists and attending to those words that are hard to learn and retain (called 'Tough Ones'). If *You Can Spell* is to help children improve their word power, then evidence of this should be found in their writing. As a user of the programme myself, I encounter children from time to time who diligently learn their spelling words yet do not transfer this knowledge to their writing. These children need to work hard on reviews and be rewarded for their efforts. A weak speller works many times harder than a child who finds the skill easy to master.

Proceeding through the Mastery Sets

Once the basic routines of the programme have been established, some children tend to find fewer and fewer words that they need to learn as they proceed through a Mastery Set. For such children, it could be that that the regularity of the programme achieves a transfer of learning as they form generalisations, or perhaps they recognise that paying closer attention to print in general enables them to remember the spelling of words more easily. I have suggested that such children be moved on quickly to complete the Set they are working on; this speed can be achieved through the teacher testing them on only the harder and more irregular words in the remaining lists. Spelling is a competence that should not be hindered by a programme that restricts what a child is 'allowed' to learn.

Working with the activities

There have been misunderstandings about the purpose of the activities in the pupils' books. As explained in this Teacher's Guide they are used to reinforce the basic concepts underpinning the *You Can Spell* programme. They are there to encourage the children to visualise word form, to locate their own error points within words ('finding hardspots'), and to memorise letter order. The focus of the activities in the first four books is on the skills required to remember and retain spelling. In this Teacher's Guide for Mastery Sets 5 to 8 the same emphases continue; however, they are enhanced by the inclusion of vocabulary activities that are implied in the Exploring Language requirement of *English in the New Zealand Curriculum*.[1]

I hope that teachers will continue to enjoy the security that the *You Can Spell* series has brought to classroom language programmes and that children will benefit from it for all of their written language activities. Please let them enjoy the antics of Mr D and his friends and the challenging puzzles sprinkled throughout the books. Learning to spell should not be a dull and lifeless daily routine.

Peter De Ath
Moana, Westland
March 2001

[1] Ministry of Education, 1995

Introduction

Research findings

In 1984 I was engaged as a research affiliate by the University of Canterbury to investigate the characteristics of proficient spellers. One of the outcomes of that investigation was the development of this spelling programme – *You Can Spell* – which is based upon the strategies of, and influences upon, capable spellers so that all primary school children might benefit.[2]

This programme also incorporates reliable findings from previous research. In particular, *You Can Spell* recognises the following:

1. The concept of frequency of word usage.
2. The importance of a need-centred approach to learning spelling. The more frequently a word is used, the greater the need for all children to master its spelling.
3. The need for appropriate procedures for learning spelling to be established early in a child's school career.
4. That an emphasis upon paying close attention to print has a beneficial effect upon learning to spell. Becoming aware of the visual appearance of print enables children to master the most commonly used words early in their school years. This in turn builds up a positive spelling self-concept.
5. The effectiveness of economical learning procedures which rely upon a visual attention to print, the location of the error point in a word, and the rote memorising of letter order. Proficient spellers are very economical in the systems they use to master spelling.
6. That parents/caregivers have a substantial influence in establishing the importance of spelling for their children. It seems that the traditional spelling homework has been a task which parents accept willingly and in so doing convey the importance of accurate spelling to their children. Children need to be trained to use the most appropriate learning strategies.
7. The importance of attending to spelling errors – if errors are repeated they tend to become a habit and progressively harder to eliminate.
8. That spelling, once learned, should be revised from time to time until mastery is achieved.

The research cast doubt upon the value of some widespread practices of the time.

- There is some evidence to suggest that success in spelling is attributable to visual rather than auditory sensations. Sounds within words help word recognition to some extent in the reading process, but they can cause confusion in spelling. When represented in print, many sounds can be recorded by a variety of letter combinations. The procedures in the *You Can Spell* programme discourage auditory involvement in the mastery of spelling.

- Copying words repeatedly does not appear to help students learn to spell. After the first model has been written, the practice becomes a deliberate copying exercise and no deliberate learning takes place. While copying a word is not harmful, it does not seem to contribute to learning.

- The remnants of kindergarten philosophy according to which young children develop without structured learning programmed may have contributed to the formal learning of spelling being delayed in our schools. The New Zealand Reading Recovery Programme has proved that six-year-old children can be successful in structured learning. Children can learn the spelling of a words once it is fixed in their reading basic sight vocabulary.

- Exercises involving spelling generalisations and rules have appeared extensively in schools' spelling programmes yet there is little evidence to suggest that they contribute to the development of spelling proficiency. Activities

---

[1] For a fuller account of the research, see:
De Ath, P. (1984) *Spelling Proficiency: An Investigation*. Education Department, University of Canterbury.

beyond the procedure for learning to spell in the early stages of the *You Can Spell* programme are designed to encourage closer attention to letter order, alphabetising, reviewing words already covered, generating extensions to root words and listing related words. At the more advanced levels, exercises involving generalisations are included to develop word study skills but they should not detract from the main purpose of the programme which is to help students to master the spelling of an increasing number of words.

The spelling lists

In compiling the lists of words for the eight achievement levels of the *You Can Spell* programme, the following existing lists were used:

- Arvidson, G. (1961) *Alphabetical Spelling List*. NZCER.
- Croft, C. et al. (1983) *Spell-Write*. NZCER.
- Elley, W.B. et al. (1977) *A New Zealand Basic Word List*. NZCER.
- Holdaway, D. (1972) *Independence in Reading*. Ashton Scholastic.
- New York Board of Education. (1965) *Teaching Spelling*. NYBOE.

These lists rely upon the frequency of use of words; however, they differ in the way the frequency ratings were established. Some (Elley, Holdaway) established ratings from an analysis of the words in children's reading materials, while others (Arvidson, Croft) analysed the words used in children's writing. Despite this difference the lists are remarkably similar even though some are a little dated. They all indicate that there are some 300 words used so frequently that they comprise approximately 75 per cent of all words used in print.

Getting children to learn to spell this batch of high-frequency words is the first target of the *You Can Spell* programme. By combining words used in children's reading and writing in the source lists, *You Can Spell* commences with 300 high-frequency words followed by 3470 commonly used words. The combined total accounts for approximately 95 per cent of all words used in print.

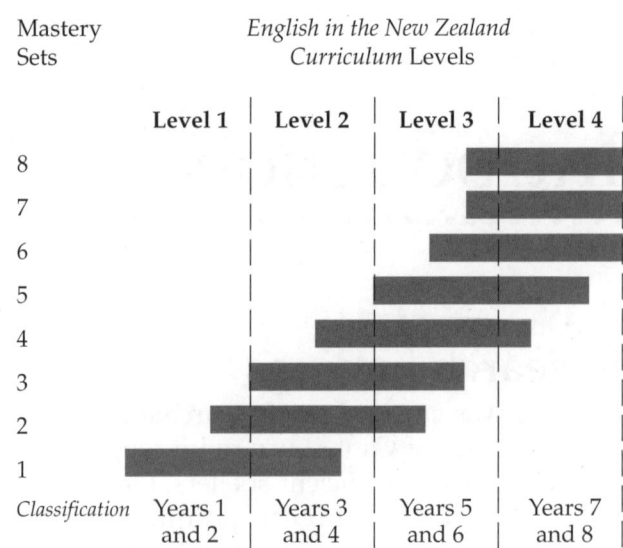

Table 1 You Can Spell *Mastery Sets per class level*

The *You Can Spell* lists have been updated to include technical, electronic, metric and commonly used Maori words. There are eight Mastery Sets of lists.

An extension book, *Now You Can Spell*, completes the series. Designed for more able spellers, its list of 700 words has been derived from specialised subject vocabularies.

The Mastery Sets

The eight Mastery Sets are sequential. Designed for learning to spell from age six, they increase in complexity to meet the needs of 12- and 13-year olds in the more advanced Sets.

However, the Sets are not prescribed by school years. Individual differences in ability and background are catered for within the programme. Table 1 illustrates how there will be several Sets operating in any class at any time. Children should proceed through Mastery Sets at their best pace, regardless of their school classification.

Teachers should not confuse the Mastery Sets with the spelling levels occurring in other programmes. The *You Can Spell* Mastery Sets are targets to be achieved. They begin with the introductory Mastery Set 1, containing the first 100 most frequently used words. Successive Sets are more demanding, as the children progress.

Sets are arranged in randomly selected learning lists which form the basis of the weekly units of the spelling programme.

Working with the lists

There are 16 words in each of the learning lists for Mastery Set 5 and 20 in the lists for Mastery Sets 6 to 8.

Not all words in a learning list are learned each week. Lists are pretested to identify only the words that the children need to master.

Testing need not be restricted to one list. Able groups can be tested over two or three learning lists in order to identify sufficient words for the week's work. This preselection of needed words limits the children's weekly learning load. Both teachers and parents/caregivers should be prepared to accept the traditional 10, 15 and 20 words per week is not necessary. It is more important to focus attention upon the 5 to 9 words (on average) that need to be mastered.

Determining a starting Set for each child

Children entering the *You Can Spell* programme at Mastery Set 1 should proceed sequentially through to Mastery Set 8. Records of progress should be kept and, when children move to another school, information about their current spelling Mastery Set should accompany them.

When the *You Can Spell* programme is being introduced for the first time, the selection tests on pp. 7–9 of this book should be used. These tests fix the children's starting Sets. A score of 25 or less indicates an appropriate starting level. These scores should ensure that the starting Sets have sufficient words in them that the children need to learn. Selection testing should occur only once in a child's experience. If, after a selection test placement, the Set does not contain sufficient challenge, the teacher should move the pupil up a Set without requiring the first Set to be completed.

Routines

The recommended routines for the *You Can Spell* programme ensure that teachers have control of their programmes at all times, and have regular feedback on student application and progress. The routines also provide for good liaison between home and school.

As indicated teachers, parents/caregivers and students should accept that the number of words to be learned each week can be quite small because they are the words that the children actually need to learn. Pupils should move through the Sets at their best rate.

The first step in the weekly routine is the pretest of a test list. Error words should be identified and then the point within the word where the error occurred. In this way attention is focused upon what has to be learned. Deviation from this strategy could fail to create a focus of learning and impede mastery.

Teachers will find that programme management is simplified when children are grouped on the same lists within a Mastery Set. Little may be gained by attempting to operate *You Can Spell* as an individualised programme. By organising the pretesting, identification and retesting procedures for groups rather than for individuals, teachers will keep in touch with the progress of all pupils.

A five-day routine should be established for classroom groups. Each session is about 15 minutes long.

Day 1

Groups are tested on the next lists in their Mastery Sets. This can be done by group monitors who have been trained to test groups below their own Mastery Set level. Training includes recognising homonyms and exemplifying which one is being tested.

Day 2

Error words are entered in the notebooks and 'hardspots' identified. This identification, indicated by underlining in red, has proved to be one of the most successful aids to learning to spell a word. The teacher should teach and revise the learning procedure regularly.

Once the children have entered their learning lists in their notebooks, and indicated the hardspots, their work should be checked for accuracy. This will avoid the possibility of a child learning an incorrect spelling from the outset.

Days 3 and 4

Children apply the learning procedure to their notebook words and work on the related activities from the pupils' books. Day 4 also requires a further learning session for homework.

Day 5

The test lists are retested with the children working in pairs. On scheduled weeks the children review their notebook words from previous lists and their accumulation of 'Tough Ones'. The pupils' book activities can be marked through group conferences with the teacher.

An alternative routine could be set up so that Days 4 and 5 bridge a weekend. Monday would always be the rest day allowing for additional time at weekends for learning the words.

Activities

The activities in the pupils' books are intended to enhance learning through focusing attention on letter order, 'hardspots' and extensions. They include puzzle grids to make the work more interesting.

Reviews, 'Tough Ones' and errors from previous levels

If mastery learning is to be achieved, children's notebook entries must be reviewed periodically to aid recall and to correct persistent errors. The 'Tough Ones' page in a child's notebook is a supplementary list of words that have not been mastered in the first instance. There are three sources for the 'Tough Ones' list: post-test errors, review test errors, and misspelled words from previous Sets.

The pupils' books for all Mastery Sets indicate to the children when a review or 'Tough Ones' test is scheduled so that they can prepare for it by relearning previous learning lists and their 'Tough Ones'. A 'Tough One' can be removed from the list only when it has been correct in two consecutive tests.

Teachers and pupils should be on the lookout for misspelled words from previous Mastery Sets occurring in day-to-day classroom writing activities. Once identified, these misspelled words should be added immediately to the weekly list. The pupils' books indicate when reviews and 'Tough Ones' tests should be taken.

Some teachers have found it more convenient to do the review and 'Tough Ones' testing in a week when the normal programme is suspended due to interruptions or holidays.

Supplementary learning words

Teachers have the flexibility to include supplementary learning words in the learning routine. These words may be drawn from a variety of sources – for example, a current centre of interest or topic, or specialised words from mathematics or other subjects. Supplementary words are added to the weekly lists in the spelling notebooks and included in the retests at the end of the week.

Another source of supplementary words is the children's written expression where they will make mistakes with names, places and events of real importance to them. Unfortunately, the testing of supplementary words set by the teacher, cannot be done in pairs because the children have the words in common. The teacher can test these words for a whole group at the end of a normal testing session.

Spelling and written expression

The ultimate test of spelling proficiency is that a writer spells words correctly in written expression. A teacher's expectation should be that the words of a current Mastery Set are being mastered and that the words of previous Mastery Sets have been mastered. Any word misspelled in written expression that has occurred in previous Sets should be a target word for the weekly list because the misspelling reveals a lack of mastery.

Misspelled words which are beyond the child's current Mastery Set should be corrected by the teacher but no further action is called for because the word will be met later in the programme.

Training in using a dictionary is a very valuable means of developing a spelling consciousness that should be emphasised whenever the children are writing.

Dictation

Dictation exercises that include words from the Mastery Sets have been included as an option in the Blackline Masters section of this *Teacher's Guide*. They are another aspect of review and each is placed after a prescribed number of lists have been learned. Misspelled words in a dictation exercise should be entered in the weekly list.

There are several advantages in using dictation exercises as a component of the spelling programme. The test of spelling proficiency is the writer's spelling accuracy in written prose. Mastery is tested because there is no time in dictation for students to consider alternative spellings. A child's level of mastery is therefore revealed. Certain aspects of the conventions of writing, punctuation, recognising the beginnings and ends of sentences and capitalisation are brought to the children's attention. Teachers will find many occasions to teach and review these conventions by working with the dictation exercises.

Technology

Children should be introduced to the technology available in the fields of spelling, word study and vocabulary extension. It is not sufficient to have just one type of dictionary available in the classroom. In addition to conventional dictionaries, there should also be a writers' dictionary.

Increasingly it is expected that children, especially those working with the more advanced Mastery Sets of *You Can Spell*, will have access to electronic spellcheckers.

Assessment and progress

Assessment of children's performance in spelling can be expressed in terms of their current position in a Mastery Set on a given date at a given age. For example:
    19/6/01   Set 5, List 20, 10 years 5 months.

Progress in spelling can be expressed by noting starting and finishing assessments over school weeks. For example:
    19/6/01   Set 5, List 20
    10/12/01   Set 6, List 14
    Interval   17 weeks
    Lists covered 29

About the Blackline Masters section

The Blackline Masters section is divided into eight parts.

1   Letters to parents/caregivers

It is important that parents/caregivers should be thoroughly briefed on the procedures and methods to be used in the *You Can Spell* programme. This is best done by explaining the programme at a meeting. The first letter invites parents/caregivers to that meeting. Inevitably, some families will not be represented so a follow-up letter is included as a means of conveying the information to those who couldn't attend. A third letter is offered for use with parents who have had some previous experience with the programme or for new parents/caregivers enrolling children through the year.

2   Training kit

There are two masters that can be used as OHP transparencies to provide a training kit for parents or a syndicate of teachers. The first emphasises the research findings underpinning *You Can Spell*. The second highlights the principal features and routines of the programme. A third transparency could be made of the 'Learning to spell a word' (p. 44) master found in the next section (Classroom aids), and used as part of the training kit.

3   Classroom aids

This section contains a wall chart model of the 'Learning to spell a word' sheet for applying the *You Can Spell* learning strategy, and models of the puzzle grids used in the various Mastery Sets.

The learning strategy sheet can be used in a variety of ways. It can be enlarged for a wall chart, used as it is and pasted into the front of a spelling exercise book, or reduced to fit a spelling notebook.

Puzzle grids can be cut and pasted into exercise books or used as a whole sheet. They will save time and keep exercise books tidy.

4   Progress graphs (score sheets)

The progress graphs (score sheets) are an important part of the weekly routine. By colouring their pretest scores in one colour and then adding their post-test gains in another, children can identify their learning gains and strive to maximise their learning with each list.

The appropriate graph should be photocopied and pasted into the child's book. Parents/caregivers should be encouraged to check the graph as the child proceeds through the Set. On the side of the graph sheet there is a record of 'Tough Ones'. This is a cumulative record which can be reduced only when a child has successfully tested on a 'Tough One' word twice.

5   Diplomas

Each diploma not only signals the successful completion of a Mastery Set but also the achievement of some other spelling milestone. Presentation by the principal at a school assembly or before the class adds to the importance of the child's achievement. Parents should also be made aware of diploma awards and may even be invited to the presentation.

6 School records

Because the *You Can Spell* programme is so well routined, teachers will not need to prepare elaborate workplans for spelling. The teacher's workplan records define the groups within the class and dates on which each is pretested. Properly maintained, these records will indicate the consistency of the class programme and the current performance position of the students throughout the year.

The pupil's record master can be photocopied onto light card and kept as a record of individual progress.

The transfer record is used when a pupil moves to another school.

7 Dictation exercises

A series of dictation exercises can be found on pp. 61–64. The dictation masters may be made into OHP transparencies and used so that children progressively learn to mark their own work. Not only should children be trained to mark their spelling errors, but they should also learn to locate the beginnings and endings of sentences, where to place apostrophes in contractions and the possessive case, and become aware of the rules for capitalisation and recording direct speech.

Almost all the words used in these exercises will have occurred in learning lists prior to the dictation being taken. However, in order to complete the context of the passage, some words do occur before their inclusion in test lists. Teachers may use their own discretion as to whether such words are to be added as supplementary words in the weekly learning lists.

Level selection tests

The following selection tests should be used only for the placement of children on a Mastery Set when they are entering the *You Can Spell* programme for the first time or when a child is returning to the programme after a time on some other spelling programme. (See p. 3 for further information about the administration of these tests.)

The Mastery Sets have been determined by the frequency of use and not by the spelling difficulty of words. For this reason selection tests cannot accurately indicate how mastery of a Set is proceeding. They can, however, be used to determine the Set at which a student should enter the programme. They should not be used for measures of assessment.

The words in each test were selected randomly from the alphabetical listing for each Set so that a representative collection of words could be achieved. Words of varying spelling difficulty are included, there are two versions of each Set Selection Test. Neither is more difficult than the other.

It should not be necessary for a child to be tested after changing schools. If both schools are using the *You Can Spell* programme, information about the child's current Set should transfer with the child.

Mastery Set 5 (Book 5)

Alternative A

act	dental
board	fit
coast	hobby
enter	lend
grand	battle
joy	castle
April	ditch
brave	fold
court	hotel
favourite	load
headmaster	belong
knock	cheese
August	dropped
bunch	fresh
dance	illness
final	lying
heat	bite
lead	citizen
baker	eastern
calf	glove

Alternative B

melt	porch
pile	root
reason	size
sew	taught
star	view
tribe	November
wrong	practice
mower	sack
playground	slip
rise	test
shining	wearing
stream	pale
tyre	puncture
needle	science
point	sore
rock	thousand
sight	whose
surely	path
upset	quiet
noon	seed

Mastery Set 6 (Book 6)

Alternative A	Alternative B
abandon	ashes
average	boss
bulldozer	character
circle	crack
daily	drug
equation	flesh
admit	guide
bathing	jeans
button	machinery
cocoa	natural
deaf	pat
excitement	produce
aid	attack
belt	brick
canary	cheer
comic	crossing
direction	eighth
fact	footpath
anxious	handle
biscuit	journey
celebrate	manager
copper	navy
divide	peas
fear	property
grabbed	absent
imagine	awake
litre	buried
motor	claws
paddock	dairy
practise	escape
article	freeze
bomb	haunt
chain	kilogram
couple	mast
driven	netting
figure	immediately
growth	photo
invitation	grade
lucky	liquid
national	muddy

Mastery Set 7 (Book 7)

Alternative A	Alternative B
abroad	ancestor
boundary	beneath
commercial	civil
appreciation	dare
deliver	dye
enjoyable	feather
flock	grateful
hail	imagination
index	knob
league	meanwhile
millimetre	noticing
occupy	payment
planned	progress
raft	result
sausage	sideways
somehow	sting
subtract	toffee
traffic	university
afford	width
attract	action
burglar	ashamed
craft	breeze
digest	continent
exchange	devil
fright	equipment
hidden	forgive
jersey	haul
lolly	invent
motorbike	linen
ourselves	mistake
political	operate
recreation	poet
seaside	realise
spice	scream
tape	sour
truth	support
waist	triangle
religious	vessel
chew	scarce
mayor	unusual

Mastery Set 8 (Book 8)

Alternative A

abundance	according		
carefully	appoint		
anonymous	battery		
bachelor	celebration		
companion	complexion		
crane	criticise		
deserve	difficulty		
encourage	equally		
fantastic	ferocious		
grammar	gymnasium		
insist	invalid		
mention	mischievous		
obedient	optimistic		
pledge	possess		
propeller	scrubbing		
risk	questionnaire		
solution	sparkle		
strategy	substance		
telescope	thorough		
vegetation	volunteer		

Alternative B

advertisement	amateur
arrangement	attach
breathing	cancer
chauffeur	cobweb
conscious	cordial
deceived	democratic
distinct	efficiency
excursion	extension
foreigner	gallop
hire	individual
liquor	martyr
motel	necessity
parallel	personally
prefer	prisoner
refugees	reservoir
siege	snatched
squirt	sticky
superior	undoubtedly
trampoline	switch
wriggle	vicinity

Test lists

Mastery Set 5 (Book 5)

List 1	List 2	List 3	List 4	List 5	List 6	List 7
act	adult	ahead	aim	allow	although	amount
bend	blackbird	beside	boot	bill	bottle	bite
billion	bone	champion	chapel	changing	circus	chase
chance	chop	change	churches	dentist	dream	dip
December	dive	dental	downstairs	deputy	flap	final
February	fit	fern	flag	film	headmaster	grill
gram	harm	grand	hate	greedy	jellies	important
idea	jar	ill	jaw	illness	loud	lid
lent	longer	less	loose	lick	nobody	nail
mower	newspaper	Ms	ninth	museum	playground	pin
piano	plain	pie	plate	pill	receive	putting
pupil	reach	pile	reason	push	sentence	sandals
safe	seed	purple	self	sale	southern	save
sliding	sort	sail	sound	slipped	throne	slippers
telephone	thirsty	slip	thousand	terrible	vanity	test
useful	web	tent	weekly	van	weigh	whanau

List 8	List 9	List 10	List 11	List 12	List 13	List 14
angry	apart	April	army	art	August	Australia
bow	blew	bowl	block	branch	blood	brave
citizen	chasing	clear	cheese	climate	chest	clock
drew	dirt	drop	dirty	dropped	diving	drove
flapping	drape	email	England	extreme	fare	filling
heal	finger	flat	finish	flies	fireman	flood
jet	guy	health	hadn't	heart	handkerchief	heat
lower	ink	join	instead	joy	item	juice
none	lie	luck	lift	lying	lion	main
pleasant	nana	noon	neat	nor	needle	northern
region	pine	plus	pipe	pocket	pit	poem
September	quack	reply	quiet	replied	rag	rice
speak	science	settle	scout	sew	seal	shade
ticket	smell	sport	smoke	spot	soil	square
weren't	thankful	tie	theatre	tied	theft	tiny
willow	view	western	village	we've	voice	wheat

List 15	List 16	List 17	List 18	List 19	List 20	List 21
awful	awoke	badly	baker	balance	bead	balloon
blow	brush	board	bull	bump	carpet	bunch
chimney	clothing	chip	coast	comb	creek	common
disease	drum	ditch	dust	easily	evil	eastern
fireplace	flour	fist	fold	follow	germ	forget
flaming	fries	gymnast	heaviest	helpful	hopping	hid
handy	he'd	hang	he'll	herring	inspector	Internet
jail	July	January	June	junk	lawn	key
lit	male	load	mark	market	melt	married
neither	nose	news	November	nut	pale	oats
pity	point	plane	pole	policeman	prize	pond
ragged	ripe	rang	rise	roam	root	roar
seam	shake	season	sharp	sheet	sight	shell
soldier	stairs	sore	stamp	star	study	steel
thick	tip	thin	tools	toss	twice	track
vote	wheel	wearing	whether	whose	wore	win

List 22	List 23	List 24	List 25	List 26	List 27	List 28
beauty	bar	bedroom	bark	bee	barn	beer
carrot	burn	cart	bush	case	cabin	castle
creep	copy	cub	corn	cutting	correct	dance
except	edge	expect	editor	fairy	eel	famous
gift	form	glove	fort	goal	fought	goat
horn	hike	hose	hind	hospital	hobby	hotel
iwi	kennel	laptop	kick	leader	kiwi	leap
lazy	kit	lead	lioness	million	mate	mix
mess	mat	mill	match	mussel	numeral	parcel
pan	October	pants	okay	parade	outdoors	pump
probably	pool	programme	porch	proud	port	pyramid
rose	rob	rot	robber	row	rock	rub
sign	she's	silly	shine	silver	shining	sir
subject	step	surely	stocking	swing	storm	tag
twins	tractor	tyre	trap	undone	tribe	unless
wrong	wing	yell	wipe	you'll	wise	you're

List 29	List 30	List 31	List 32	List 33	List 34	List 35
base	beginning	basketball	belong	bathroom	below	battle
calf	cause	calves	cave	capital	certain	careful
cost	dash	court	daughter	cream	deal	crowd
eighty	further	electric	favourite	enter	feast	especially
fresh	golden	gale	grab	gate	grain	general
honey	hug	hook	hung	hop	hut	hopped
knives	least	knock	led	lamp	lend	lap
maths	moan	matter	moon	meal	mow	meeting
pack	path	packed	peanut	pad	person	page
possible	pumpkin	post	puncture	pot	pup	practice
rocky	rug	rod	sack	roll	sad	roof
sauce	saveloy	shore	skip	standard	slid	shut
shirt	size	snatch	tap	stream	taught	struck
straight	tale	strange	Tasman	temple	tuna	trunk
trick	upper	trouble	upset	truly	upstairs	volcano
wives	you've	woke	valley	wonder	vegetables	wooden

Mastery Set 6 (Book 6)

List 1	List 2	List 3	List 4	List 5	List 6
accident	addend	agree	aircraft	atom	Auckland
account	addition	agreement	airport	atomic	bathing
bait	address	bare	barrel	barrier	bulldozer
brick	broadcast	broom	bubble	bucket	Christchurch
cheer	cheerful	cherry	chocolate	circle	claws
display	drill	distance	engineer	district	drug
fan	figure	fasten	flesh	favour	Dunedin
grapes	hammer	groan	handle	groceries	fled
information	junior	inspect	keen	invitation	harbour
lucky	material	magazine	meant	maid	kindergarten
oak	ought	oasis	ourselves	oatmeal	measles
pinch	polar	pipi	polite	pirate	oven
question	relax	rake	remind	range	popular
rule	scene	scrap	serve	scratch	rent
ruler	scenery	secret	service	shock	several
score	separate	secretary	settler	shook	speed
surf	special	smooth	speech	snake	taste
towards	tank	surface	tar	surround	twig
whip	trimmed	towel	tunnel	trade	Wellington
within	woollen	whistle	worm	willing	worry

List 7	List 8	List 9	List 10	List 11	List 12
bay	cent	burst	axe	butterfly	bury
berry	centimetre	cliff	beef	cloud	buried
berries	century	cocoa	bushes	computer	button
burnt	decimal	coconut	clever	donkey	clown
clerk	harden	coffee	commerce	ferry	effort
divide	kilogram	dollar	committee	guard	fond
fear	kilometre	fellow	community	journal	haunt
growl	kindness	growth	dump	keyboard	knee
joke	litre	jolly	float	march	message
manufacturing	medicine	marble	harvest	monitor	owner
obey	metre	object	kiss	offer	pour
plantation	overalls	plastic	member	player	reward
rapidly	population	raw	owl	reader	rugby
screen	report	scrub	position	search	soccer
snap	shadow	smile	return	swell	shark
swam	spider	smiling	shape	social	spoke
swum	tax	socks	spirit	transport	tear
terrify	ugly	sweep	taxi	video	tennis
trail	weight	tramp	umbrella	wine	union
winding	worse	windmill	worth	x-ray	wrap

List 13	List 14	List 15	List 16	List 17	List 18
contest	beetle	beg	belongings	belt	bench
danger	cabbage	cabinet	calendar	camel	capture
dangerous	collar	colony	comfortable	comic	concrete
double	driven	dozen	empty	drawn	enemy
fever	driver	eighth	exam	exciting	energy
guide	electricity	fierce	examination	excitement	equation
journey	fool	gum	footpath	finally	forgotten
mare	healthy	judge	heater	halves	fraction
officer	lace	mask	ladder	jungle	height
pleasure	midnight	orchestra	mineral	mast	law
referee	paddle	plough	paddock	orchard	medication
section	powder	refuse	practise	poison	mischief
solid	ribbon	seek	rifle	regular	pain
sunny	shelter	seventh	shift	senior	prepare
sunrise	spill	soup	stable	space	roast
sunset	spilt	tame	tomato	tan	shopping
sunshine	spread	technical	tomatoes	tore	stage
sword	temperature	technology	usual	torn	term
tray	unknown	treat	vine	treasure	type
winner	wrist	wire	yawn	witch	valuable

List 19	List 20	List 21	List 22	List 23	List 24
curly	actually	Bible	anxious	annoy	ant
escape	bent	candle	appear	area	anywhere
forced	canary	copper	ballet	biscuit	blanket
freeze	control	current	birth	canoe	caravan
frost	deck	eve	cane	cosy	cone
froze	garage	forward	costume	daily	cottage
frozen	governor	happily	decorate	everywhere	dial
herd	government	happiness	gather	freedom	gaze
language	however	hiding	geography	hoof	hunter
missile	lightning	lawyer	history	hooves	jandals
palace	musical	mist	human	learnt	jeans
press	peak	panel	limb	model	limp
roller	proper	prevent	narrow	panic	nasty
shoulder	salmon	rooster	peas	peach	perfect
skate	single	shovel	property	price	protect
skating	strip	stall	sandwich	rough	sandy
ski	tiger	though	sink	shower	slave
snowball	underneath	vase	struck	steam	stuff
therefore	understand	wolf	tight	thread	timber
various	wave	wolves	weak	verb	weapon

List 25	List 26	List 27	List 28	List 29	List 30
ancient	alive	aid	artist	adventure	afterwards
arrow	apron	article	ashes	attack	assembly
bleed	blind	blink	bloom	bomb	central
carpenter	carriage	celebrate	cement	check	crew
count	cradle	couple	crab	crack	direction
dairy	dictionary	dam	destiny	damp	experience
ewe	dragon	exercise	dining	extra	goose
fuel	geese	furniture	goldfish	holy	immediately
hoe	husband	hollow	goodnight	length	lock
leather	liquid	legend	imagine	millennium	necessary
machine	manage	moment	list	moss	net
machinery	manager	nation	nature	neighbour	netball
modern	native	national	natural	neighbourhood	netting
paragraph	perfume	pardon	nearby	paste	period
print	prove	prison	perhaps	process	punch
route	saucer	rush	public	rusty	scarf
shown	sleepy	sickness	saving	stock	slippery
steal	success	stiff	slim	terrified	super
throat	toast	thrown	suit	thumb	toe
violin	we'd	visitor	wedding	wagon	welcome

List 31	List 32	List 33	List 34	List 35
adopted	admit	absent	actual	abandon
author	attention	avenue	average	awake
boom	boss	bother	breast	breath
chain	chalk	character	charge	chart
criminal	crop	crossing	crown	cruel
dancing	disappoint	discover	disco	deaf
explain	fact	factory	fail	faint
future	grabbed	gala	grade	gang
homework	indoors	honest	industry	honour
lettuce	lonely	level	lose	liberty
motive	navy	motor	maybe	muddy
niece	phone	patch	notice	patrol
nephew	photo	project	pilot	promise
pat	pillow	rainy	purpose	robot
produce	pure	raincoat	record	rocket
saddle	scientist	safety	recorder	sailor
signal	smart	simply	scissors	sincerely
stole	supper	stomach	supply	straw
thus	togs	tick	touch	tidy
wake	whale	wasp	whenever	waste

Mastery Set 7 (Book 7)

List 1	List 2	List 3	List 4	List 5	List 6
ability	activities	aboard	activity	absence	advantage
appearance	ashore	appreciate	aside	appreciation	association
bored	breeze	borrow	bridle	bound	bud
collection	consider	college	contain	colt	continent
dawn	design	daylight	destination	death	destroy
dyeing	embroidery	eagle	enjoyable	earlier	dwelling
fax	flash	feather	flax	female	entertain
gorilla	grease	graceful	guest	gradually	flight
iceberg	improvement	iceblock	including	icy	gumboots
kingdom	knowledge	kneel	koala	knelt	increase
majority	measure	mammal	medal	manner	labour
multiplication	nuclear	mumps	noticing	murder	memory
overseas	passenger	owing	pattern	oxygen	nowhere
pray	private	prayer	problem	pressure	payment
refreshments	repeat	regard	reptile	relation	product
seaside	shelf	seldom	shellfish	sense	rescue
spare	stack	spear	stain	spice	shelves
swept	thief	swift	thieves	system	starch
triangle	umpire	tripped	unconscious	trousers	thorn
verse	warmth	vessel	waterfall	vinegar	wealth

List 7	List 8	List 9	List 10	List 11	List 12
ache	advice	achieve	afford	acquainted	agriculture
argue	atmosphere	argument	attend	arrange	attract
boundary	bulb	boyfriend	bullet	brain	bundle
comical	continue	command	cough	commercial	council
deed	development	degree	devil	consideration	dew
earliest	entertainment	earn	entirely	delicious	envelope
fertile	flock	fireworks	flow	easier	fluffy
grandparents	gymnastics	grateful	habit	fisherman	hail
idle	indeed	imaginary	independence	grave	independent
knight	lack	knit	lame	imagination	lantern
manufacturing	merrily	mass	metal	knitting	meter
mystery	nuisance	naturally	nylon	matches	obtain
oyster	peace	palm	pear	necklace	pepper
pretend	production	primary	professor	parrot	progress
relative	resist	relay	respect	relief	restaurant
serious	shepherd	servant	shiny	settlement	shiver
spin	state	splash	statement	splendid	stationary
tape	thoughtful	target	thrifty	tease	throughout
trout	understood	trust	underwater	truth	undressed
violent	wealthy	violet	weave	voyage	weekend

List 13
acre
arrest
brake
complete
delighted
elect
flame
gravel
importance
knob
mathematics
nervous
particular
principal
religion
shady
split
teaspoon
tube
waist

List 14
airline
automatic
burglar
counter
diamond
equal
folk
hairy
index
laser
method
occasion
permission
protection
result
shone
stationery
thunder
unfortunate
wharf

List 15
action
arrival
brass
concert
deliver
election
flannel
graze
impossible
knot
mayor
noisy
partner
principle
religious
shaking
spoil
tender
tune
wander

List 16
alarm
backwards
butcher
courage
diary
equipment
foolish
ham
injured
league
mighty
occasionally
photograph
provide
rotten
shopkeeper
statue
tide
unhappy
wharves

List 17
active
ashamed
breathe
condition
dense
electronic
flare
grazing
improve
knotted
meanwhile
normal
passage
prisoner
remain
share
sprain
tenth
twelfth
wardrobe

List 18
alert
bacon
calm
craft
diaries
event
ford
handful
injury
lemon
millilitre
occupation
phrase
puzzle
rubbish
sideways
steer
tidied
unidentified
whatever

List 19
alligator
camera
crank
difference
dissatisfaction
exactly
foreign
harness
instance
lemonade
millimetre
occupied
pigeon
pyjamas
ruin
silence
stem
tiptoe
uniform
wheelbarrow

List 20
ancestor
beneath
choir
cure
drawer
explosion
gain
highway
jersey
lollies
monster
operation
poet
rainbow
scale
smoking
strike
tough
unusual
wreath

List 21
alike
bakery
cardboard
crawl
difficult
example
forgive
hatch
instrument
license
millionaire
occupy
pioneer
quality
runner
silent
sting
title
unit
wherever

List 22
angel
blade
chorus
curtain
drown
express
gasp
hobbies
jewel
lolly
moth
opposite
poetry
rare
scarce
somehow
student
tour
vacant
wreck

List 23
aloud
bandage
careless
crept
digest
excellent
fountain
haul
intelligent
lime
military
occur
pitch
quantity
safety
silk
stir
toffee
unite
whisper

List 24
angle
blast
civil
cushion
drunk
extremely
gentle
hockey
jewellery
lounge
motion
ordinary
police
realise
scary
snapped
subtract
tow
vacuum
yacht

List 25
altogether
barley
cast
crime
disagree
excite
frame
hawk
invent
limit
miner
octopus
planet
quarrel
salad
skirt
stool
toilet
universe
wicked

List 26
ankle
blossom
classroom
damage
due
fade
gentleman
horrible
judging
luggage
motorbike
organ
policewoman
recent
scramble
sniff
subtraction
tower
value
zebra

List 27
amaze
baseball
ceiling
cripple
disappear
exchange
freight
heaven
invention
linen
minister
odd
planned
radar
salute
skull
stoop
tongue
university
widow

List 28
announce
boil
cloak
dare
dull
fairies
giggle
horror
justice
lung
mount
organise
political
recipe
scream
soak
succeed
traffic
vanish
zero

List 29
amazing
bathe
celery
crisp
discovery
exhibit
fried
hedgehog
inventor
lipstick
mirror
onion
planning
raffle
satisfied
slam
stranger
toothbrush
unlucky
width

List 30
anyhow
booklet
clover
darkness
duty
fairly
glitter
household
kangaroo
magnet
mountainous
owe
postage
recognise
screen
sofa
successful
trapped
variety
zone

List 31
ambulance
beam
chapter
crumb
distant
expensive
friendship
heel
irrigation
lizard
mistake
opera
platform
raft
satisfy
slice
strap
toothpaste
unpack
worn

List 32
apology
bonfire
coach
dart
dwarf
fallen
golf
huge
attractive
kauri
magnetic
movies
ourselves
poster
recreation
screw
sour
suggest
traveller
varnish

List 33
amuse
bean
cheap
crust
division
elementary
explode
fright
hero
jacket
loaf
operate
playcentre
rail
saucepan
slime
stray
torch
untie
worst

List 34
apologise
border
collect
data
dye
fancy
goodness
hurricane
kettle
mainly
multiply
outline
powerful
rectangle
seagull
spade
support
treaty
vehicle
whoever

List 35
amusement
behaviour
chew
cupboard
dodge
explore
furnish
hidden
jealous
loaves
moisture
operating
playful
railway
sausage
smack
strength
total
untied
wound

Mastery Set 8 (Book 8)

List 1
absolutely
announcement
automobile
cannibal
colourful
creak
democratic
ecstasy
expression
funeral
impatient
management
muscles
pause
preparation
rehearse
signature
stadium
superior
training

List 2
abundance
annual
awfully
canvas
column
creature
deny
efficiency
extend
furious
include
manoeuvre
musician
peaceful
prepared
reliable
similar
stalk
supermarket
trampoline

List 3
accept
anonymous
awkward
capacity
combine
cricket
deposit
efficient
extension
furry
inconvenient
manuka
mysteries
pearl
preparing
remainder
siren
stallion
supplies
transferred

List 4
accidentally
Antarctica
bachelor
capsule
commission
criticism
descending
elbow
extraordinary
gallop
indicate
marae
mysterious
peculiar
presence
remark
situated
stare
surgeon
travelling

List 5
accommodate
anxiously
bacteria
carefully
companion
criticise
descent
element
facsimile
gem
individual
marriage
navigation
penguin
preserve
remembrance
situation
staring
surrender
tremble

List 6
accommodation
appeal
badge
cassette
comparatively
crocodile
describe
embarrass
faith
generally
industries
martyr
necessarily
perform
president
repetition
skateboard
starve
survive
tremendous

List 7
accompanied
appetite
banner
catalogue
compare
cuddle
description
embarrassment
faithful
genius
industrious
marvellous
necessity
personal
previous
represent
skeleton
starving
suspicious
trial

List 8
accompany
apply
banquet
catastrophe
compass
cultivate
deserve
emergency
false
Germany
influence
massive
nevertheless
personally
pride
representative
skilful
steady
swallow
troop

List 9
according
applying
barbecue
catches
compel
cordially
desire
encourage
familiar
gigantic
initial
matinee
nickel
perspiration
prisoner
reserve
slammed
steak
swamp
tropical

List 10
accurate
appoint
bargain
caterpillar
competition
correspondence
desperate
encyclopedia
fantastic
giraffe
innocent
mechanical
noble
persuade
privilege
reservoir
smelt
stereo
sway
turtle

List 11
acknowledge
appointment
battery
cease
competitor
courageous
dessert
endeavour
fascinated
grammar
inquire
memories
numerous
physical
proceed
responsibility
snatched
stew
sweat
trying

List 12
acknowledgement
appreciated
beautifully
celebration
complain
courteous
determined
engage
fashion
glory
insist
memorable
nursery
physician
procedure
resources
sneak
sticky
sweater
undoubtedly

List 13
acquaintance
approach
beggar
cemetery
complexion
courtesy
devote
enormous
fatigue
grocery
instant
mention
obedience
pickle
profit
revolver
sneezed
stitch
switch
unforgettable

List 14
acrobatic
appropriate
believing
centennial
composition
crackers
diameter
enthusiasm
fault
guarantee
interfere
mere
obedient
picnicking
prominent
revolution
society
stolen
syllable
unnecessary

List 15
adjective
approval
benefit
ceremony
concerned
crane
difficulty
entrance
favourable
guardian
intermediate
merely
observe
pledge
pronunciation
rhyme
softball
storey
sympathy
urge

List 16
admission
approximately
bluff
certainty
conductor
crashes
dinghy
equally
feature
guerilla
interrupt
messenger
occurred
pneumonia
propeller
rhythm
solar
stormy
symphony
useless

List 17
advance
apricot
bossy
certificate
conference
crayfish
directly
equipped
ferocious
guitar
introduce
microphone
occurrence
poisonous
proportion
risk
solo
straighten
tablet
vain

List 18
advertise
aquarium
boulder
chamber
confidence
curiosity
disagreeable
errand
fiery
gymnasium
introduction
microscope
official
policy
propose
sacrifice
solution
stranded
tariff
vary

List 19
advertisement
arose
bounce
championship
confident
curious
disappointment
error
filthy
hamburger
invalid
minimum
opinion
polished
prosperous
satisfactorily
solve
strategy
task
varying

List 20
advise
arrangement
branches
changeable
conjunction
curve
disaster
establish
financial
handsome
investigate
mischievous
opportunity
pollution
punish
satisfactory
somersault
strawberry
telescope
vast

List 21
aerial
artificial
breathing
charm
conqueror
cycle
discipline
eventually
flavour
hangi
invisible
miserable
optimistic
portion
purchase
sauna
soul
stretch
television
vegetation

List 22
affair
ascend
brief
chauffeur
conscience
cylinder
discussion
evidence
foal
happiest
irresistible
missionary
ordinarily
possess
quantities
scarcely
source
struggle
temper
vengeance

List 23
affect
assistance
brilliant
chemist
conscious
debt
disguise
exaggerate
foggy
heavier
Italian
misspelled
ore
possession
questionnaire
schedule
souvenir
stumble
temperament
vicinity

List 24
affectionately
assistant
Britain
chemistry
consent
deceive
dissatisfied
examine
footsteps
helicopter
justify
modelling
organisation
possibility
quilt
scrubbing
spaceship
stupid
temporary
victory

List 25
agent
associate
chopped
considerably
decision
distinct
exclaim
forecast
herald
laboratory
monotonous
original
pounce
radish
saxophone
secure
sparkle
submarine
territory
vigorous

List 26
agreeable
assume
bruise
Christian
constitution
declaration
distinguish
excursion
forehead
heroes
librarian
monotony
originally
practical
rattle
seize
specimen
substance
theory
villain

List 27
aisle
assure
bulletin
circumstance
construction
declare
distributed
exhausted
foreigner
hinge
likelihood
moral
otherwise
practically
recite
sensible
spectators
subtle
thorough
volcanoes

List 28
alcohol
astonished
bureau
civilisation
container
decoration
dolphin
exhibition
forfeit
hire
likely
mortgage
pace
praise
recommend
separation
spotted
suddenly
thoroughly
volunteer

List 29
alphabet
athlete
burrow
claim
content
defeat
doubt
exist
forgetful
hostage
liquor
mosquito
Pacific
preach
reduce
sergeant
sprang
sufficient
threaten
weird

List 30
altitude
athletics
cafeteria
cleanliness
continually
defence
doubtful
existence
former
homesick
literature
motel
parachute
precede
reference
series
sprinkle
suggestion
thrilled
whitebait

List 31	List 32	List 33	List 34	List 35
amateur	amazement	American	analyse	anniversary
Atlantic	attach	attachment	attempt	authority
campaign	canal	cancer	candidate	candy
closely	clump	cobweb	coffin	colonel
convenience	conversation	co-operation	copies	cordial
definitely	delicate	delight	delightful	demand
dutiful	earnest	earthquake	economic	economical
expedition	expense	expensive	experiment	explanation
formula	fortunate	fragile	freckles	frequently
humorous	icicle	ignorance	imitation	immigrants
locate	loneliness	losing	make-up	magnificent
mould	moveable	movement	mule	municipal
parallel	parliament	particularly	pastime	patient
precious	prefer	preference	preferred	prejudice
referred	refrigeration	refugees	regretted	reign
severe	shearing	shrieking	siege	signalled
squash	squeak	squeeze	squid	squirt
suitability	suitable	suitcase	sunbathe	superintendent
tickled	tournament	trace	tragically	tragedy
worthy	worried	wrestle	wrestling	wriggle

Answers to activities in pupils' books

Mastery Set 5 (Book 5)

List 1
1. hopeful, careful, useless, hopeless, careless
2. bend, idea, gram, pupil, mower, billion
3. loan, borrow, lent, lend
4. Across: pupil, telephone, sliding, chance
   Down: useful, piano, December
5. January, February, March, April, May, June, July, August, September, October, November, December
6. kilogram, milligram

List 2
1. bl<u>a</u>ckb<u>i</u>rd, n<u>e</u>wsp<u>a</u>per
2. seed, chop, bone, dive, thirsty
3. There is a review test in List 3 Exercises.
4. Across: reach, jar, plain, thirsty
   Down: adult, newspaper
5. longer, longest, harmful, harmless, chopped, chopping
6. blackboard, blackmail, blacksmith

List 3
1. gram (1), grand (3), greedy (5), grill (7), grab (32), grain (34)
2. grand, dental, tent, pile, slip, champion
3. dental, change, ahead, beside, purple
4. They have a final or silent 'e'.
   chance, safe, telephone
5. slipping, slipped, slipper
   You double the 'p'.

List 4
1. upstairs
2. weekly, jaw, loose, plate, flag
3. chose, loose, lose, choose
4. Across: ninth, weekly, self, downstairs
   Down: sound, reason, flag, churches
5. slippers, gumboots, sandals
6. hated, hating, hateful, selfish, selfless, reasoning, reasonable

List 5
1. i<u>ll</u>ness, terri<u>b</u>le, gr<u>ee</u>dy, chang<u>ing</u>, a<u>ll</u>ow
2. chill, skill, drill, spill, grill
3. change, ill, greed, slip
4. Across: slipped, film, terrible, allow
   Down: dentist, museum, bill, pill, push
5. car, bu<u>s</u>, truck, bike
6. Spelling is a very important skill.

List 6
1. all + though, head + master, no + body, play + ground
2. headmaster, throne, dream, jellies, nobody
3. jelly, baby, lady
4. Across: although, circus, headmaster
   Down: weigh, playground, nobody, southern
5. northern, eastern, western

List 7

1. pin, grill, save, bite, dip, test, chase, final
2. sandals, nail, final, lid, bite
3. Most children like the puzzles in this book.
4. Across: sandals, putting, test, save
   Down: slippers, bite
5. biting, chasing, saving
   You leave out the final 'e'.
6. dipped, dipping, pinned, pinning
   You double the final consonant.

List 8

1. flap, anger, low
2. jet, citizen, drew, speak, willow
3. lower, ticket, angry, region, weren't
4. flew, crew, stew, chew, slew, screw
5. heal, heel (In that order.)
6. September

List 9

1. blink, brink, stink, clink, chink
2. nana, quack, blew, view, smell
3. bl<u>e</u>w, sci<u>e</u>nce, cha<u>sing</u>, thankfu<u>l</u>, li<u>e</u>
4. Across: smell, finger, thankful, pine
   Down: dirt, science, lie
5. thankful, smell, science

List 10

1. replied, replying
2. bo<u>w</u>l, plu<u>s</u>, he<u>a</u>lth, west<u>er</u>n, j<u>oi</u>n
3. At noon we all join in and play sport.
4. Across: sport, western, April, luck
   Down: drop, health, settle
5. April, noon, email, settle, noon
6. plus, clear, bowl, noon, sport

List 11

1. dirtied, dirtying
2. theatre, village, army, quiet, finish
3. quite, quiet (In that order.)
4. Across: finish, theatre, hadn't, smoke
   Down: instead, cheese, block, village
5. England
6. shock, stock, flock, frock, knock

List 12

1. drop, fly, reply, tie
2. heart, pocket, extreme, replied, flies
3. dro<u>pp</u>ed, fl<u>ies</u>, we<u>'</u>ve, clim<u>ate</u>, extr<u>e</u>me
4. Across: pocket, tied
   Down: spot, dropped, branch, climate
5. A dictionary is useful for checking spelling.

List 13

1. scare, flare, spare, share, glare
2. lion, handkerchief, chest, rag, pit
3. seal, soil, item, lion, voice, fare
4. The letter 'e' (14 times).
5. Diving, fireman, handkerchief
6. August

List 14

1. shade, juice, clock, heat, poem, main, rice
2. clock, juice, flood, Australia, shade
3. mane, main (In that order.)
4. Across: square, northern, flood, wheat
   Down: Australia, tiny
5. oats, barley, corn
6. emptying, cold, southern

List 15

1. fireplace, fireman
2. a<u>w</u>ful, dis<u>ease</u>, n<u>ei</u>ther, sold<u>ier</u>, fla<u>ming</u>
3. At school you can learn many things.
4. Across: seam, lit, disease
   Down: soldier, jail, handy, chimney
5. chimney, handy, pity

List 16

1. drummed, drumming, pointed, pointing
2. brush, drum, flour, male, stairs

3 flour   mail   male
flower (In that order.)
4 Across: awoke, clothing, drum
Down: flour, he'd, point
5 a = 4, e = 9, i = 6, o = 5, u = 4
6 flour   point   stairs
male   shake

List 17
1 stitch   witch   switch
hitch   pitch
2 season   ditch   sore
news   thin
3 The Spelling Feast was fun. I hope we get another one in *Book 6*.
4 Across: thin, wearing, January, board
Down: season, news, badly, ditch
5 Summer   Autumn   Winter
Spring
6 gymnastics   gymnasium

List 18
1 fall   unfold
blunt OR flat (*Music*)
2 baker   sharp   coast
rise   tools
3 stamp   coast   sharp
baker   tools
4 whether, weather (In that order.)
5 drake   ram   buck
rooster (cockerel)
gander   boar

List 19
1 ease   easier   easiest
2 comb   policeman   roam
follow   sheet
3 market   balance   whose
herring   helpful
4 Across: comb, star, balance, toss, policeman
Down: bump, market, whose
5 peanut   coconut   walnut
6 sheen   sheep   sheer

List 20
1 evil   lawn   germ
pale   study   bead
2 twi<u>c</u>e   germ   carp<u>e</u>t
stud<u>y</u>   inspect<u>o</u>r
3 creek, site, creak, sight (In that order.)
4 Across: lawn, carpet, evil, sight
Down: twice, hopping, melt
5 slice   spice   splice
nice   mice
6 This list has an evil germ hopping inspector in it.

List 21
1 balloon   common   married
shell   steel
2 balloon   shell   pond
steel   forget
3 lunch   crunch   hunch
munch   punch
4 Across: bunch, married, pond
Down: common, forget, shell
5 pool   lake   sea
ocean

List 22
1 beautiful   painful   wrongful
2 twins   gift   pan
lazy   subject
3 If you get the wrong answer you will have to try again.
4 Across: except, probably, rose, twins, lazy
Down: carrot, beauty, wrong
5 except   subject   beauty
wrong   rose
6 The letter 'r' (7 times).

List 23
1 ledge   hedge   dredge
sledge   wedge
2 wing   hike   copy
edge   pool
3 edge   tractor   burn
wing   step
4 barring   matting   robbing
stepping
The final consonant is doubled.
5 nest   den   burrow
dam
6 August   January

List 24
1 cart   cub   glove
hose   lead   mill
pants   rot   tyre
yell
2 cub   silly   yell
hose   glove
3 One sentence about rapid breathing, the other about trousers.
4 Across: lead, programme
Down: bedroom, glove, pants, mill, tyre
5 bedroom   laptop

List 25
1 okay   robber   stocking
2 edit<u>o</u>r   robber   por<u>ch</u>
liones<u>s</u>   sto<u>c</u>king
3 We must learn as many words as we can.

4 Across: bush, stocking, corn
     Down: porch, bark, shine
  5 chick   slick   trick
     quick   stick
  6 robber   porch   hind
     lioness   trap

List 26
  1 cutting   leader   mussel
     parade   undone
  2 swing   bee   silver
     leader   fairy
  3 le<u>a</u>der million   pro<u>u</u>d
     fai<u>r</u>y be<u>e</u>
  4 Across: case, hospital, bee
     Down: proud, parade, cutting, leader
  5 bee   case   goal
     proud   row   swing
  6 You'll   proud   goal
     million   silver

List 27
  1 correct   wise   outdoors
  2 eel   barn   storm
     port   mate
  3 Stop the people from earth using words
     immediately.
     Or: Stop the earth people from using words
     immediately.
  4 Across: fought, tribe, storm, shining
     Down: wise, outdoors, eel
  5 Most likely options are: wind   gale
     rain   hail   flood

List 28
  1 beer   leap   pump
     goat   rub   mix
     sir   tag
  2 leap   dance   famous
     goat   parcel
  3 castle   dance   parcel
     hotel
  4 horses   sheep   cows
     deer   donkeys   mice
  5 prince   princess   duke
     duchess
  6 Egypt

List 29
  1 eighty   honey   rocky
     They end with a 'y' vowel.
  2 straight   honey   possible
     base   knives
  3 ba<u>s</u>e   po<u>ss</u>ible ho<u>n</u>ey
     ca<u>lf</u>   sau<u>ce</u>

  4 Across: knives, straight, shirt, pack
     Down: wives, trick, eighty, Maths
  5 base   honey   wives
     shirt   maths
  6 The letter 's' (11 times).

List 30
  1 hug   tale   pumpkin
     beginning   least
  2 begi<u>nn</u>ing mo<u>a</u>n you<u>'v</u>e
     c<u>au</u>se pumpkin
  3 furher   leas   pah
     ale
  4 Across: beginning
     Down: upper, pumpkin, golden, moan
  5 You've   tale   dash
     further   path

List 31
  1 snatch   matter   trouble
     strange   packed
  2 strange   knock   court
     shore   post
  3 stranger   strangest   strangely
  4 Across: strange, packed, post, rod, calves,
     trouble
     Down: court, basketball
  5 basketball   electric   matter
     packed
  6 You will soon be at the end of *Book 5*.

List 32
  1 belong   peanut   upset
     basketball   bathroom
  2 puncture   cave   tap
     moon   upset
  3 <u>T</u>asman fav<u>ou</u>rite pun<u>cture</u>
     d<u>au</u>ghter val<u>ley</u>
  4 Across: skip, puncture, peanut
     Down: hung, sack, upset, belong
  5 slave   behave   shave
     Dave   crave
  6 The letter 'a' (10 times).

List 33
  1 steam   stream   team
     ream   scream
  2 wonder   lamp   gate
     bathroom   hop
  3 capital   stream   wonder
     cream   enter
  4 meal   cream   enter
     temple   gate
  5 Wellington   Canberra   London
     Paris

List 34

1. deal, feast, grain, hut, lend, mow, pup, sad, slid, ta__u__ght, tuna
2. vegetables, upstairs, below, feast, ta__u__ght
3. person, grain, vegetables, upstairs, certain
4. Across: deal, vegetables, hut, mow
   Down: taught, below, upstairs
5. upstairs, downstairs
6. stain, strain, chain, train, drain

List 35

1. crowd, trunk, shut, struck, page, lap
2. car__e__ful, ba__tt__le, stru__ck__, especia__ll__y, gen__e__ral
3. general, volcano
4. Across: general, crowd, careful, battle
   Down: meeting, especially, lap
5. battle, especially, hopped, meeting, wooden
6. Congratulations!! You have now completed *Book Five*. Well done!!

Mastery Set 6 (*Book 6*)

List 1

1. ruler, cheer, score, bait, surf, fan
2. tow__a__rds, o__a__k, a__cc__ount, inf__o__rmation, s__u__rf
3. dis–, in–
4. accident
5. Bait, pinch, Oak, Fan, Cheer
6. We hope you enjoy working with *Book 6*.

List 2

1. drill, ought, scene, tank
2. broadcast
3. material, polar, cheerful, address, figure, hammer
4. Across: material, ought
   Down: hammer, separate, broadcast
5. addition, figure
6. untrimmed

List 3

1. grown, Bare, Bear, groan (In that order.)
2. where, whine, which, whip
3. whi__s__tle, sec__r__etary, dist__a__nce, s__u__rf__a__ce, maga__z__ine
4. cherry, broom, secret, oasis, inspect
5. agree

List 4

1. aircraft, airport, ourselves
2. barrel, bubble, engineer, keen, settler, speech, tunnel
3. barrel, settler, tunnel, bubble, service
4. Lessons make playtime more attractive.
5. barrel
6. ourselves, engineer, chocolate

List 5

1. in-vit-a-tion
2. snake, atom, district, range, bucket
3. Christchurch, Christine, Clark Street, October, Friday
4. shock, favour, bucket, atomic, pirate
5. lady, factory, bunny
6. The letters 'a' and 'i'. (Both 13 times.)

List 6

1. kin – der – gar – ten
2. tasted, tasting, tasty
3. k.p.h, port, more than one, trouble, well liked
4. screen, scrub, several, shadow, shape, smile, smiling, snap, socks, speed, spider, spirit, swam, sweep, swum
5. influenza, pneumonia, bronchitis

List 7
1. Bury, Berry (In that order.)
2. berry   berries   divide   obey   winding
3. manufacturing   plantation   rapidly
4. Across: clerk, winding, trail, terrify, snap
   Down: burnt, plantation, growl
5. disobey   unwinding
6. rapid   terror

List 8
1. information   question   addition   invitation   plantation   population
2. hard – en   shad – ow   re – port   kind – ness
3. centime*tre*   me*di*cine   over*all*s   pop*u*lation   sha*d*ow   w*o*rse
4. worse   litre   shadow   report   medicine
5. centimetre   century   kilogram   kilometre
6. spider

List 9
1. cliff   coffee   dollar   fellow   jolly   sweep   windmill
2. Raw, roar (In that order.)
3. coconut   plastic   fellow   marble   dollar
4. Good exercise is not always something in a maths book.
5. windmill

List 10
1. shaped   shaping   shapely
2. har – vest   mem – ber   re – turn
3. commerce
4. isn't   what's   a boy's shirt   you'll   mustn't
5. circle   triangle   octagon   hexagon   rectangle
6. howl   growl   scowl   prowl

List 11
1. transplant   transship   transform
2. butterfly   keyboard
3. keep safe   increase in size   involving people   log of events   water vapour
4. march   mare   mask   message   midnight   monitor
5. fly   moth   mosquito   wasp   ant
6. antisocial

List 12
1. paw, pore, Pour, poor (In that order.)
2. cricket   softball   hockey   netball
3. effort   buried   reward   tennis   button
4. Across: shark, message, fond, buried
   Down: effort, reward, tennis
5. unbutton   unwrap

List 13
1. sunrise   sunset   sunshine
2. manger   ranger   stranger
3. d*ou*ble   dang*er*ous   sec*ti*on   refer*ee*   g*ui*de
4. referee   solid   contest   journey   sword
5. safety   loser
6. dangerous   referee   officer

List 14
1. electric – ity
2. beetle   cabbage   collar   fool   paddle   ribbon   spill
3. driver   cabbage   collar   healthy   unknown
4. In this room the last sharp pencil died yesterday.
5. sleeve   cuff   lapel   seam   hem
6. wrong   wreck   wrinkle   wrap   wriggle

List 15
1. geology   zoology   biology   meteorology   psychology
2. first   second   third   fourth   fifth
3. fierce   orchestra   judge
4. Mr Brown's cow. The cycle rack. The Red Sea. Angela's mother. Lake Taupo. The green water.
5. refuse

List 16
1. footpath
2. com – for – ta – ble   min – er – al   cal – en – dar

3 miner's desire   expression of tiredness
   test   climbing plant
   relocate
4 finally   footpath   forced
   forgotten   fraction   freeze
   frost   froze   frozen
5 uncomfortable   unstable   unusual
6 heater   mineral   practice

List 17
1 excite   final
2 pleasure
3 regular   finally   poison
   senior   camel   orchard
4 Across: camel, senior, jungle, exciting
   Down: treasure, comic, belt, torn
5 The spelling witch.
6 poison   regular   senior
   comic   treasure

List 18
1 Each word has three syllables.
2 capture   enemy   valuable
   forgotten
3 en<u>e</u>my   cap<u>ture</u>   p<u>ai</u>n
   valu<u>able</u> concr<u>ete</u>   equ<u>a</u>tion
4 bench   fraction   roast
   enemy   law
5 preview   preschool   prejudge
   preoccupy   prepaid

List 19
1 dangerous
2 heard, herd (In that order.)
3 escape   frozen   shoulder
   frost   forced
4 You will never break records if you only buy tapes.
5 freeze   froze   frost
   frozen   skate   skating
   ski   snowball
6 language   various

List 20
1 however   understand
2 actually   finally
3 lightening
4 lightning   lightening (In that order.)
5 A new house. Every Wednesday. Anzac Day. March the fifth. The wheel on Mrs Smith's Honda.
6 underage   underestimate   underwear
   underfed   underground

List 21
1 copper   current   happily
   happiness   rooster   stall
2 happy   happier   happiest
3 reddish metal   the night before
   thin sheet   horse box   light fog
4 ancient   annoy   ant
   anxious   anywhere   appear
   area   arrow   eve
   everywhere   ewe
5 hoe   rake   spade
   fork

List 22
1 strong   week
2 death   berth
3 ballet   costume   decorate
   appear   narrow
4 Across: birth, peas, geography
   Down: tight, history, decorate, property
5 disappear   wide   float
   loose
6 geography   history

List 23
1 everybody   everything   everyone
   somewhere   nowhere   anywhere
2 area   learnt   peach
   steam   thread
3 bis<u>cui</u>t   d<u>ai</u>ly   fr<u>ee</u>dom
   mode<u>l</u>   lear<u>n</u>t   pani<u>c</u>
4 steam   canoe   daily
   shower   everywhere
5 yacht   punt   dinghy
   jetski
6 rough   panic   everywhere
   cosy

List 24
1 blank – et   car – a – van   per – fect
   tim – ber
2 geography   history   property
3 jandals   jeans   cottage
   caravan   blanket
4 I love my aunt. She always buys me socks for my birthday.
5 castle   shack   flat

List 25
1 hasn't   o'clock
   Maria's bicycle   The ladies' hats
   The baby's toys
2 bleeding   counting   dairying
   hoeing   machining   stealing

3 ancient   modern
4 violin   modern   arrow
  leather   machine
5 you   root   steel
6 recount   refuel   reprint
  reroute

List 26
1 successful   successfully   successive
2 goose
3 state the facts   fluid   hold carefully
  deal with   indigenous
4 pardon   paste   perfume
  perhaps   period   prison
  process   prove   public
  punch
5 uncle   boy   Pa
  prince   duke   lad
6 The letters 'e' (16 times) and 'a' (14 times).

List 27
1 cel – e – brate   fur – ni – ture
  ex – er – cise
2 visit   visited   visiting
3 couple   pardon   prison
  moment   article
4 Across: stiff, thrown, national, celebrate
  Down: furniture, couple, article
5 shrink   drink   slink
  clink   blink

List 28
1 imagined   imagining
  imagination   imaginative
2 current   prevent   absent
3 dining   artist   nature
  ashes   wedding
4 goldfish   goodnight   ashes
  nearby   suit
5 whale   trout   eel
  crayfish   octopus
6 unnatural   unimaginative unsuitable
  unartistic

List 29
1 terrific   terrifies   terrify
2 bomb   thumb   limb
3 length   attack   process
  adventure
4 School is useful for having holidays.
5 bomb   check   crack
  damp   length   moss
  paste   stock   thumb
6 bombs   extras   wagons
  mosses

List 30
1 assembly   immediately necessary
  slippery
2 few   flew   dew
  new   blew
3 crews   geese   toes
  punches   scarves
4 Jade Stadium. I climbed Mount Cook. Bill sailed the seven seas. The Titanic sank in the Atlantic Ocean. Mary is coming on Tuesday.
5 assembly   goose   immediately
  necessary   netball   netting
  slippery

List 31
1 producer   produced   producing
  production
2 ex – plain   crim – in – al
  ad – opt – ed sig – nal   mo – tive
3 intention   manufacture
  time yet to come   message
  took unlawfully
4 future   lettuce   lose
  motive   niece   notice
  phone   produce   promise
  pure   purpose   stole
5 aunt or uncle   brother or sister
  mother and father
6 homework

List 32
1 disappear   distasteful dislocate
  disengage   disbelieve
2 attention   boss   disappoint
  grabbed   indoors   pillow
  supper
3 indoors   pillow   admit
  attention   supper
4 Across: disappoint, pure
  Down: indoors, supper, pillow, phone, attention
5 pencil   crayon   felt pen
  charcoal
6 The letter 't' (11 times).

List 33
1 object   subject   reject
  inject   project
2 absent   safety   honest
3 gala   simply   factory
  character   discover
4 wasp   gala   absent
  tick   level
5 character   honest   gala
  project

List 34
1. whenever — maybe
2. re – cord – er — av – er – age
   in – dus – try — pur – pose
   act –u – al
3. pilot — recorder — notice
   charge — scissors
4. Spelling lists are not good for you, they just get harder and wear out your brains.
5. disco — notice — pilot
   purpose — record — scissors
   supply
6. actual — charge — scissors
   maybe — record

List 35
1. waist
   waste, Waist (In that order.)
2. awake — cruel — tidy
3. liberty — faint — sincerely
4. rocket — patrol — straw
   chart — sailor
5. sincere — nearly — quickly
   truly — finally

Mastery Set 7 (Book 7)

List 1
1. abilities — faxes — gorillas
   majorities — spares
2. appear
   disappear — appearing — appeared
3. collection — dawn — kingdom
   overseas — ability
4. ability — aboard — absence
   activities — activity — appearance
   appreciate — appreciation — ashore
   aside
5. iceberg — overseas — seaside
   daylight — iceblock — shellfish
   waterfall
6. multiplication — triangle

List 2
1. activity — active
   activate — deactivate — inactive
2. around — aboard — accustom
3. shelf — stack — umpire
   design — thief
4. embroidery — breeze — consider
   thief — private
5. consider — nuclear — activities
   measure — umpire
6. act – iv – it – ies — con – sid – er
   im – prove – ment — pas – sen – ger

List 3
1. mam – mal — ves – sel — bor – row
   col – lege
   Syllables usually split between double letters.
2. college — daylight — eagle
   feather — iceblock — mammal
   mumps — prayer — spear
   vessel
3. seldom — owing — aboard
   tripped — borrow
4. eagle — owing — appreciate
   seldom — graceful
5. Across: prayer, appreciate, daylight
   Down: aboard, eagle, graceful

List 4
1. activity — bridle — destination
   flax — guest — koala
   medal — pattern — problem
   reptile — shellfish — stain
   thieves — waterfall
2. capable — reliable — likeable
3. unconscious — destination — aside
   guest — including
4. Nicola said"I'd rather have a music lesson than do these spelling exercises."
5. enjoyable — unconscious — including
   problem
6. pipi — cockle — mussel
   paua

List 5
1. prettier — uglier — funnier
   nastier
2. appreciate — early — gradual
   relate
3. bound — pressure — manner
   system — sense

4 They were under pressure to explain their absence earlier this morning.
5 bound   colt   death
  knelt   sense   spice
6 School time should not interrupt holidays.

List 6
1 advantageous courageous humorous
  dangerous   nervous
2 destroy   entertain   nowhere
3 increase   wealth   thorn
  labour   rescue
4 gum – boots   no – where
  grand – parents   boy – friend
  under – stood   fire – works
  under – water
5 continent   entertain   dwelling
  advantage

List 7
1 latest   prettiest   ugliest
  biggest   smallest   scruffiest
2 spin   pretend   ache
  idle   deed
3 comical   fertile   pretend
  relative   violent
4 boundary   earliest   knight
  relative   tape
5 boundary   comical   earliest
  grandparents mystery relative
  serious   violent
6 earliest   pretend   idle
  fertile

List 8
1 state
2 painful   hopeful   beautiful
  successful skilful
3 peace   continue   advice
  nuisance   production
4 gymnastics nuisance   merrily
  atmosphere
5 Across: development, continue, advice, entertainment
  Down: nuisance, production, wealthy
6 development production continue
  merrily

List 9
1 degrees   masses   primaries
  splashes   violets
2 mass   palm   degree
3 grateful   primary   mass
  trust   command

4 Next week we're going to the Students' Convention in Martinborough.
5 sprint   discus   high jump
  javelin

List 10
1 underwater
  underwear   underarm   understudy
  understand   underground
2 insane   indirect   inactive
  indefinite
3 professor   entirely   thrifty
  weave   bullet
4 professor   statement   respect
  independence
5 entirely   nylon   shiny
  thrifty
6 A sandwich always tastes better at a picnic.

List 11
1 match
2 image
  imagining   imagined
  imaginative   imaginatively   unimaginative
  unimaginatively
3 truth   easier   delicious
  settlement   matches
4 unacquainted untruth   unequal
5 agriculture   independent   stationary
  stationery   Mathematics   particular
  automatic   unfortunate   impossible
6 The vowel 'e' (18 times).

List 12
1 due   metre   counsel
  stationery
2 dependent   dressed   moving
  repel
3 attract   obtain   lantern
  hail   restaurant
4 stationary   undressed   dew
  pepper   agriculture
5 Throughout   weekend   Council
  obtain   restaurant

List 13
1 break   principle   waste
2 waste, break, principle, brake, principal, waist (In that order.)
3 delighted   importance   principal
  religion

4 knob   elect   gravel
   arrest   split
5 nerv<u>ou</u>s   a<u>cre</u>   religi<u>o</u>n
   grav<u>e</u>l   i<u>mporta</u>nce
6 Across: Mathematics, religion, arrest, complete, delighted
   Down: importance, elect, shady, split

List 14
1 unequal   bald   fortunate
2 lasers   airlines   indices
   wharves
3 counter   permission   index
   automatic   folk
4 "Quick!" said Jim. "Jump in the boat. We're off to Brighton."
5 ruby   emerald   sapphire
   amethyst
6 burglar   counter   method
   thunder   airline

List 15
1 concert   tune
2 knot   not
   mayor   mare
   principle   principal
3 principle   impossible   noisy
   wander   deliver
4 ele<u>c</u>tion   may<u>or</u>   de<u>l</u>iver
   ac<u>tio</u>n   i<u>mpossi</u>ble
5 Homework is only good when teachers forget to set it.

List 16
1 alarm   butcher   courage
   diary   equipment   ham
   league   photograph   shopkeeper
   statue   tide   wharves
2 diary   mighty   occasionally
   unhappy
3 foolish   mighty   provide
   diary   injured
4 forward   inward   outward
5 condition   occupation   dissatisfaction
   operation
6 unhappy

List 17
1 sixth   eighth   eleventh
   fourteenth   thirty-ninth
2 electronic   electrode   electrify
   electromagnetic   electrostatic
3 remain   share   breathe
   dense   active
4 sprain   normal   twelfth
   meanwhile   wardrobe

5 jacket   jeans   jersey
   jandals
6 ashamed   improve   prisoner
   passage   wardrobe

List 18
1 oc-cu-pa-tion   un-i-dent-if-ied
   in-jur-y   what-ev-er
2 diary   tidy   identify
   They end with a 'y' vowel.
3 unidentified   craft   phrase
   alert   rubbish
4 ca<u>l</u>m   puzz<u>l</u>e   tid<u>ie</u>d
   handf<u>ul</u>   mil<u>l</u>ili<u>tre</u>
5 Across: millilitre, tidied, handful, whatever
   Down: alert, unidentified, ford, lemon

List 19
1 occupier   rider   listener
2 differ
   different   indifferent   differently
   indifferently   indifference
3 ruin   occupied   silence
   exactly   uniform
4 You'll need your calculator, a pencil, rubber and ruler for this test.
5 coffee   cocoa   orange juice
   cola
6 alligator   millimetre   pyjamas
   pigeon   silence

List 20
1 beneath   gain   unusual
   tough
2 an-ces-tor   ex-plo-sion   op-er-a-tion
   un-us-u-al
3 gain   scale   cure
   monster   poet
4 explo<u>s</u>ion   u<u>n</u>usual   monst<u>er</u>
   bene<u>a</u>th   hi<u>gh</u>way
5 I have a pet toad. My mother doesn't like it.
6 The consonant 'r' (11 times).

List 21
1 gasp   gentle   hatch
   haul   hawk   hobbies
   hockey   instrument   intelligent
   invent   jewel   jewellery
2 crawling   forgiving   hatching
   licensing   occupying   pioneering
   stinging
3 pioneer   forgive   license
   difficult   quality
4 example   unit   license
5 crawl   hatch   sting

List 22
1. drown, rare, scarce, somehow, vacant
2. angels, choruses, lollies, moths, hobbies
3. curtain, jewel, gasp, vacant, wreck
4. angel, express, tour, blade, drown
5. tour, wreck, scarce, rare, poetry, hobbies
6. opposite, poetry, angel, jewel, vacant

List 23
1. senseless, motherless, powerless, restless, hopeless
2. crept, haul, lime, pitch, silk, stir
3. unite, excellent, careless, whisper
4. digest, fountain, occur, wh<u>i</u>sper, band<u>a</u>ge
5. Across: silk, crept, intelligent, lime, safety, unite
   Down: careless, stir, military, excellent, digest, toffee
6. aloud, allowed, haul, hall

List 24
1. extremely, hockey, jewellery, ordinary, scary
2. example, express, excellent, extremely
3. extremely, cushion, lounge, motion, realise
4. If three boys had three books where would you put the apostrophe in the boys' books?
5. brooch, necklace, wedding ring, pendant, bracelet

List 25
1. disappear, discontent, displace, discontinue, disobey
2. exciting, excited, excitingly, excitedly, excitement, unexcited, unexciting, unexcitingly
3. wicked, invent, quarrel, cast, disagree
4. al<u>t</u>ogether, di<u>s</u>agree, univer<u>s</u>e, th<u>ere</u>, plan<u>e</u>t, wic<u>k</u>ed, oct<u>o</u>pu<u>s</u>
5. lettuce, tomato, cucumber, radish
6. Have you ever tried to vacuum up baked beans? It makes your mum angry.

List 26
1. submarine, substandard, substation, subject, subside
2. class-room, gentle-man, motor-bike, police-woman
3. scramble, due, luggage, blossom, damage
4. … begins with a vowel.
5. heaven, hedgehog, horrible, horror, household, linen, lipstick, luggage, lung, magnet, radar, raffle, recent, recipe, recognise
6. worth, cost, pay, cheap, bargain

List 27
1. college, school, seminary
2. amaze, disappear, odd, planned, stoop
3. planned, exchange, amaze, disappear, cripple
4. freight, odd, skull, minister, university
5. sheets, pillowcases, towels

List 28
1. vanish, zero, cloak, scream, succeed
2. boil, cloak, dare, dull, lung, mount, scream, soak
3. recipe, succeed, announce, dare, soak
4. fair<u>ies</u>, organi<u>s</u>e, horr<u>o</u>r, su<u>cc</u>eed, justi<u>ce</u>
5. Across: cloak, announce, horror, boil, succeed, political
   Down: fairies, lung, recipe, zero, giggle
6. political, succeed, organise, justice, vanish

List 29
1. strange, strangely, strangest
2. hedge, hog, lip, stick, tooth, brush
3. width, crisp, exhibit, satisfied, slam
4. "We've had enough of these tricky exercises haven't we?" sighed Alice.

5	boil	roast	stew
	hangi	barbecue	
6	celery	onion	clover

List 30
1. hopelessness cheerfulness faithfulness
   happiness tiredness
2. successful fairly
3. recognise variety zone
   screen booklet
4. dark<u>ne</u>ss tra<u>pp</u>ed mount<u>ai</u>n<u>ou</u>s
   su<u>cc</u>essful d<u>u</u>ty
5. Our teacher is psychic. He knows when mum does my homework.

List 31
1. chapter friendship lizard
   mistake platform toothpaste
2. fellowship comradeship craftsmanship
3. slice beam expensive
   distant mistake
4. inexpensive dissatisfy unattractive
   unscrew derail unwound
5. expensive attractive amusement
   sausage
6. message expensive platform
   chapter

List 32
1. apologise suggestion attractively
   hugely
2. apologies dwarfs varnishes
3. suggest huge dart
   poster movies
4. varnish screw dwarf
   traveller coach
5. attractive dart traveller
   suggest huge bonfire
6. e a o i u

List 33
1. bean cheap crust
   fright loaf rail
   slime stray torch
   worst
2. expensive coward best
   tie multiplication
3. crust stray operate
   slime elementary
4. unt<u>ie</u> sa<u>uce</u>pan <u>o</u>p<u>e</u>rate
   w<u>o</u>rst playcent<u>re</u>
5. Across: operate, jacket, saucepan, torch, slime
   Down: worst, playcentre, crust, explode

List 34
1. collect goodness hurricane
   kettle seagull support
2. dye fancy mainly
   multiply treaty
3. treaty data border
   dye hurricane
4. "I just can't get these right," said Nicola. "I'll have to use that girl's dictionary."
5. dye
   Dye, die (In that order.)
6. data datum

List 35
1. loaf wolf hoof
2. cupboard moisture railway
   sausage total
3. moisture amusement explore
   furnish jealous
4. dew mist condensation
   drizzle
5. I wrote a letter today. I think it was P.

Mastery Set 8 (Book 8)

List 1
1. adjustment   detach   government
2. expressed   expressing   expressive
   expressionless   expressible   expressly
3. superior   impatient   stadium
   pause
4. absolutely   abundance   accept
   accidentally   accommodate   announcement
   annual   anonymous   Antarctica
   anxiously   automobile   awfully
   awkward
5. ecstasy   expression   efficiency
   extend   efficient   extension
   elbow   extraordinary   element
   funeral   furious   furry
   facsimile
6. impatient

List 2
1. rely
   relies   relying   relied
   unreliable   reliability   unreliability
   reliant   reliably   reliance
2. awe   create   efficient
   fury   music   peace
   prepare
3. annual   furious   reliable
   extend   column
4. canvas   trampoline   musician
   abundance   column
5. prepared   creature   peaceful
   musician   abundance
6. stalk

List 3
1. in-con-ven-i-ent   awk-ward
   man-u-ka   cap-a-cit-y
2. supply, –ies   mystery, –ies   extend, –sion
   acceptance   depositor
3. transferred   combine   remainder
   anonymous
4. anon<u>y</u>mous   prep<u>a</u>ring   transfe<u>rr</u>ed
   pe<u>a</u>rl   capa<u>c</u>ity
5. Across: accept, furry, inconvenient, mysterious
6. Down: efficient, transferred, cricket, deposit

List 4
1. Antarctica   bachelor   capsule
   commission   criticism   elbow
   gallop   marae   presence
   remark   stare   surgeon
2. bachelor   surgeon
3. surgeon   capsule   criticism
   presence
4. "Oh!" said Nicola. "I can't possibly learn all these words."
5. bachelors   criticisms   maraes
   peculiarities
6. descending   travelling   bachelor
   situated   peculiar

List 5
1. remember   accommodation   preservation
   navigate   marry
2. cafeteria   malaria   petunia
   hysteria   insomnia   suburbia
3. facsimile   bacteria   accommodate
   individual
4. a<u>ccomm</u>odate   facs<u>i</u>mile   individ<u>ua</u>l
   st<u>ar</u>ing   remem<u>br</u>ance
5. swap   swallow   swindle
   swear   swirl
6. Jem's favourite activities are BMX racing and listening to music

List 6
1. badges   industry   martyrs
2. skate – board
   cupboard   keyboard   overboard
3. faith   perform   appeal
   describe
4. badge   faith   starve
5. crocodile   turtle

List 7
1. appetite   banner   catalogue
   cuddle   description   embarrassment
   genius   necessity   skeleton
   trial
2. faith
   faithfully   faithless   faithlessness
   unfaithful   unfaithfulness
3. catalogue   faithful   banner
   genius   industrious
4. previous   embarrassment   catalogue
   skeleton   starving
5. skull   spine   femur
   hip   shoulder
6. unaccompanied unfaithful

List 8
1. sk<u>ill</u>   person   company
   emerge
2. One: false   pride
       troop
   Two: apply   banquet
       compass   deserve
       massive   skilful
       steady   swallow

	Three:	cultivate	influence
		Germany	
3	catastrophe	massive	accompany
	apply		
4	person**a**lly	ski**l**ful	ban**q**uet
	a**cc**ompany	catastroph**e**	
5	Wellingtonians	Welsh	Dutch
	Mexicans	Balinese	
6	Across: catastrophe, troop, banquet, emergency
	Down: cultivate, accompany, pride, steady, nevertheless

List 9

1	bar-be-cue	com-pel	gi-gan-tic
	trop-ic-al	pris-on-er	catch-es
2	perspire	encouragement	
	reservation	imprison	
3	matinee	Perspiration	
	cordially	compel	
4	Nicola said that we shouldn't miss her band's concert.
5	lead	copper	aluminium
	iron	zinc	

List 10

1	bargain	caterpillar	competition
	turtle	giraffe	
	They are all nouns.		
2	caterpillar	competition	
	correspondence	encyclopedia	mechanical
3	persuade	fantastic	competition
	innocent		
4	co**rr**esponden**c**e	priv**i**lege	a**pp**oint
	ca**t**erpillar		
5	The students really like to listen to Nicola's band.

List 11

1	batteries	desserts	stews
	memories	memory	
2	dessert	grammar	proceed
3	courageous	numerous	fascinated
	appointment		
4	numerous	cease	proceed
	courageous	appoint	
5	response	beauty	nurse
	stick	doubt	grocer
	necessary (necessitate)		difficult
	mere		
6	We don't think that Nicola likes the Review reminder rodent.

List 12

1	knowledge : ac : ment	doubt : un : ed : ly
	celebrate : tion	beauty : ful : ly
2	creature	exposure	moisture
	pleasure	pressure	
3	fashion	insist	physician
	complain	courteous	
4	nursery	insist	sweater
	sticky	celebration	
5	skulk	lurk	creep

List 13

1	discourtesy	disobedience	
	unforgettable		
2	courtesies	beggars	cemeteries
	groceries	switches	
3	approach	profit	instant
	unforgettable		
4	comple**x**ion	snee**z**ed	c**o**urtesy
	enorm**ou**s	fat**i**gue	
5	sauce	jam	mayonnaise
	dressing		
6	Across: unforgettable, beggar, grocery
	Down: instant, complexion, sneezed, profit

List 14

1	compose	picnic	enthuse
	interference		
2	prominent	appropriate	obedient
	revolution		
3	stolen	society	fault
	guarantee		
4	"Will you be going to tonight's show?" asked Freda.
5	shortbread	chocolate	Shrewsbury
	wafer		
6	believe	compose	picnic
	revolve		

List 15

1	adaptable	admirable	debatable
	honourable	comfortable	
2	adjective	approval	benefit
	ceremony	crane	difficulty
	entrance	guardian	pledge
	pronunciation	rhyme	softball
	storey	sympathy	urge
3	storey	benefit	approval
	merely		
4	ben**e**fit	pronun**c**iation	g**u**ardian
	rh**y**me	fav**ou**rable	
5	How do you know if there is a spelling mistake in a dictionary?

List 16
1. ap-prox-i-mate-ly   cer-tain-ty
   din-ghy   e-qual-ly   stor-my
   sym-pho-ny
2. admit   certain   conduct
   equal   message   occur
3. messenger   stormy   feature
   certainty
4. admission   advance   apricot
   aquarium   advertisement   arrangement
5. symphonies   solos   sacrifices
   solutions   strategies   somersaults
   strawberries
6. Generally American spelling uses '–ize' where English spelling uses '–ise'.

List 17
1. conference   occurrence
   emergence   impudence   obedience
   preference   subsidence   turbulence
2. cer-tif-i-cate   pro-por-tion   in-tro-duce
   mic-ro-phone   con-fer-ence
3. certificate   proportion   tablet
   vain   bossy
4. apricot   ferocious   microphone
   occurrence   vain
5. clarinet   violin   saxophone
   trumpet
6. o e i a u

List 18
1. introduce   proposition   variation
2. bolder
   boulder   bolder (In that order.)
3. sacrifice   stranded   fiery
   aquarium
4. e<u>rr</u>and   g<u>y</u>mnasium   sacri<u>f</u>ice
   disagr<u>ee</u>able   a<u>q</u>uarium
5. Across: curiosity, fiery, official, chamber
   Down: confidence, vary, tariff, sacrifice, gymnasium

List 19
1. confident   strategy   solve
   advertisement   error
2. "I wish we'd less work to do in these books," announced Bill.
3. curious   polished   invalid
   championship   satisfactory
4. advert (ad)   champ   burger
5. invalid
6. championship   minimum   satisfactorily
   disappointment   confident

List 20
1. establish   branches   pollution
   disaster
2. arrange   change   finance
   satisfy   pollute
3. disaster   handsome   arrangement
   establish
4. s<u>o</u>mersault   o<u>p</u>portunity   mischi<u>e</u>vous
   c<u>u</u>rve   chang<u>e</u>able
5. enormous   huge   gigantic
   colossal
6. Have you ever found a word that didn't have a vowel?

List 21
1. cycle   flavour   hangi
   portion   purchase   sauna
2. visible   visibility
3. flavour   artificial   discipline
   stretch
4. possess   misspelled   possession
5. invisible   discipline   optimistic
   eventually   television

List 22
1. irresponsible   irrepairable   irregular
   irreverent
2. sauce
   sauce   source (In that order.)
3. struggle   possess   chauffeur
   evidence   ascend
4. missionary   ordinarily   discussion
   source   struggle
5. duckling   kitten   gosling
   piglet   calf
6. e i a o u

List 23
1. con–
   contract   concussion   conflict
   condition   concern
2. pos-ses-sion   tem-per-a-ment   as-sist-ance
   ex-agg-er-ate
3. debt   conscious   schedule
   ore
4. po<u>ss</u>ession   vi<u>c</u>inity   bri<u>ll</u>iant
   vict<u>o</u>ry   mi<u>ss</u>pelled
5. Across: temperament, disguise, chemist, ore
   Down: debt, possession, misspelled, co<u>ns</u>cious
6. conqueror   chauffeur   missionary
   assistant   Italian   agent
   associate   herald

List 24
1. assistant, Britain, chemistry, consent, footsteps, helicopter, organisation, possibility, guilt, spaceship, victory
   'Britain' is the proper noun.
2. satisfied, satisfy
3. possibility, organisation, stupid, deceive
4. The last of Mike's pencils are on the table next to that girl's ruler.
5. botany, biology, physics, zoology, aeronautics, astronomy, geology

List 25
1. radishes, laboratories, agents, associates, territories
2. unchopped, indecision, indistinct, unoriginal, insecure
3. territory, monotonous, considerably, associate
4. as**soc**iate, vig**or**ous, te**rr**it**o**ry, spar**k**le, deci**s**ion
5. Nicola is our swimming champion. She is a really good athlete too.
6. *Photocopy results for classmates to have fun with.*

List 26
1. fore – head, bridgehead, masthead, bedhead, overhead, arrowhead, blockhead
2. assumed, assuming, unassuming, assumption, assumingly, unassumingly, assumedly
3. villain, bruise, theory, excursion
4. librarian, excursion, agreeable, originally, distinguish
5. librarian, practical, substance, specimen, declaration
6. monotony, Monopoly

List 27
1. I'll alter him.
2. recitation, declaration, construct, assurance
3. bulletin, thorough, spectators, construction, aisle
4. volcanoes, declare, sensible, bulletin, spectators
5. aisle, hinge

List 28
1. mountaineer, engineer, auctioneer, mutineer
2. bureau, dolphin, forfeit, mortgage
3. mortgage, bureau, forfeit, exhibition
4. th**o**roughly, mor**t**gage, sep**a**ration, forf**ei**t, dec**o**ration
5. Egyptian, Greek, Roman, Byzantine, Aztec
6. Across: thoroughly, hire, container
   Down: spotted, decoration, volunteer, dolphin

List 29
1. merciful, wonderful, dreadful, graceful
2. Antarctica, German, Italian, Britain, Christian, Pacific
3. hostage, sufficient, content, weird
4. For Miri's fruit salad we need some apples, grapes and peaches.
5. beetle, sandfly, dragonfly, weta
6. excursion, exhausted, exhibition, exist, existence, forehead, foreigner, forfeit, forgetful, former

List 30
1. continually, doubtful, homesick, precede, thrilled
2. altitude, athletics, cleanliness, existence, parachute, reference, suggestion
3. cafeteria, cleanliness, whitebait, motel, continually, homesick
4. continu**ally**, par**a**chute, prec**e**de, ref**e**rence, lit**e**rature
5. Jeremy's learned to spell aeronautical. Now he wants to be an airline pilot.

List 31
1. close, define, duty, humour, refer, suit
2. closely, locate, amateur, humorous, precious
3. expedition, precious, severe, convenience, worthy
4. convenience, humorous, suitability, expedition, formula
5. squash
6. campaign, locate, tickled, severe, parallel

List 32

1. con-ver-sa-tion　re-frig-er-a-tion
   a-maze-ment　tour-na-ment
   lone-li-ness
2. worried　expense　earnest
   delicate　suitable
3. moveable　fortunate　prefer
   suitable　delicate
4. shearing　parliament　moveable
   squeak　delicate
5. move
   remove　removed　removing
   remover　removal　movement
   moveability　unmoved　unmoving

List 33

1. suitcase　earthquake　cobweb
   They are compound words and nouns.
2. One – American.
3. fragile　ignorance　attachment
   refugees
4. co-operation　attachment　particularly
   preference　refugees
5. Across: delight, preference, ignorance, refugees
   Down: expensive, fragile, cancer, trace

List 34

1. analysis　imitate　preference
   wrestler
2. One:　mule　seige　squid
   Two:　attempt　coffin　copies
   　　　freckles　make-up　pastime
   　　　sunbathe　wrestling
3. candidate　attempt　experiment
   pastime　wrestling
4. "No! I need six boys' boots," said the coach.
   "Don't you understand plain English?"
5. mock　sham　copy
   substitute　artificial
6. economic　imitation　sunbathe
   preferred　pastime

List 35

1. economy　frequent　explain
   signal
2. rain　rain
3. prejudice　magnificent　tragedy
   explanation
4. anniversary　prejudice　immigrants
   tragedy　economical
5. You have completed *Book Eight*.
   Congratulations!

Blackline Masters

1 Letters to parents/caregivers

Letter 1

Dear

This year our children will be using the *You Can Spell* programme to learn their spelling. The most important part of this programme is the method children use to master their spelling words.

Research shows that the home and the school are partners in reinforcing correct spelling and so it is important that we should all be encouraging children to use the same learning method. To help you understand the *You Can Spell* programme we invite you to a meeting to be held:

on (date) ....

at (time) ....

in (venue) ....

We do hope you can attend because the information we have for you will help your child to make progress in spelling.

Signed:

Letter 2

Dear

I was sorry that you could not attend our recent parent meeting about spelling. Here are some of the points covered. I think they are important and I hope that you find them helpful as .... [name of child] proceeds through the *You Can Spell* programme this year.

- The programme is based on a five-day cycle. On Day 1, lists of words are tested and marked. The children enter their error words in their notebooks. On Days 2, 3 and 4 the children learn their words and use them in spelling activities at school. On Day 4, usually Thursday, they also learn their words again for homework. On Day 5 the learning lists are retested.
- Persistent errors (called 'Tough Ones') are frequently brought up for relearning and review.
- The learning method we want your child to use has been developed after thorough research. Children should identify their error points in words. We call this 'hardspotting'. Your child should be able to tell you exactly where he or she went wrong in spelling the word and also tell you what the correct version is. Children should be able to visualise the form of the word with eyes closed and recite the letters in order. Only after these two important steps have been taken should the child write the words once to ensure that correct learning has taken place.
- This method is the one being used at school and is recommended for home use to ensure consistency in our partnership. No other additions should be made to the method – especially NOT activities such as sounding out words or writing out words ten or so times. Spelling is a highly visual skill. Sounding out words only confuses and copying them many times serves very little purpose.
- *You Can Spell* is arranged in eight Mastery Sets. Set 1 is begun in the junior classes and Set 8 should be achieved by most children by the end of Year 8. Each Mastery Set is a level of proficiency for which a near 100% accuracy is required. A diploma is issued on the satisfactory completion of each level.

I believe that all children can make progress in spelling providing the right methods and routines are followed. Please feel free to contact me with any queries you may have on this important matter.

Signed:

Letter 3

Dear

This year our children will be using the *You Can Spell* programme to learn their spelling. The most important part of this programme is the method children use to master their spelling.

Research shows that the home and the school are partners in reinforcing correct spelling and so it is important that we should all be encouraging children to use the same learning method. The following points should help you understand how the programme works.

- The programme is based on a five-day cycle. On Day 1, lists of words are tested and marked. The children enter their error words in their notebooks. On Days 2, 3 and 4 the children learn their words and use them in spelling activities at school. On Day 4, usually Thursday, they also learn their words again for homework. On Day 5 the learning lists are retested.

- Persistent errors (called 'Tough Ones') are frequently brought up for relearning and review.

- The learning method we want your child to use has been developed after thorough research. Children should identify their error points in words. We call this 'hardspotting'. Your child should be able to tell you exactly where he or she went wrong in spelling the word and also tell you what the correct version is. Children should be able to visualise the form of the word with eyes closed and recite the letters in order. Only after these two important steps have been taken should the child write the words once to ensure that correct learning has taken place.

- This method is the one being used at school and is recommended for home use to ensure consistency in our partnership. No other additions should be made to the method – especially NOT activities such as sounding out words or writing out words ten or so times. Spelling is a highly visual skill. Sounding out words only confuses and copying them many times serves very little purpose.

- *You Can Spell* is arranged in eight Mastery Sets. Set 1 is begun in the junior classes and Set 8 should be achieved by most children by the end of Year 8. Each Mastery Set is a level of proficiency for which a near 100% accuracy is required. A diploma is issued on the satisfactory completion of each level.

I believe that all children can make progress in spelling providing the right methods and routines are followed. Please feel free to contact me with any queries you may have on this important matter.

Signed:

2 Training kit

Spelling research findings

- ➤ Children *need* to learn the most commonly used words as early as possible.

- ➤ A person's spelling self-concept is established at an early age.

- ➤ Parents/caregivers have a powerful influence over establishing the importance of correct spelling.

- ➤ Spelling is a highly visual skill depending more on the sense of sight than on hearing.

- ➤ Home and school must share a united approach to the way children learn their spelling.

- ➤ Some techniques may hinder spelling development.

The *You Can Spell* programme

Eight Mastery Sets based on the frequency of usage of words.

Learning lists for each Set are pretested to locate the words a child *needs* to learn.

Class programme based on a five-day cycle with frequent reviews of previously learned words.

Persistent errors are corrected and the words learned again.

Involves homework and motivation from parents/caregivers.

Has a very strict learning procedure

Rewards achievement of each Set.

Starts in junior classes.

Anticipates proficiency by the end of Year 8.

3 Classroom aids

Learning to spell a word

Compare what you wrote with the correct spelling of the word.
You wrote: **importence**
The correct spelling is: **importance**

Locate where you went wrong. (We call this the hardspot.)

Underline the hardspot. (This is what you must learn.) **import<u>a</u>nce**

Close your eyes.

Imagine you can see the word.

Recite the letters in order as you would say a phone number.
i-m-p-o-r-t-a-n-c-e

Test yourself by writing the word from memory.

Repeat this method several times with each word.

Will it work?

It did for me.

You must do it quite a few times.

That's true

How long will you keep it?

It has a lifetime guarantee if you review your words often.

Puzzle grids
You Can Spell Mastery Set 5

List 1 (p. 6)

List 2 (p. 7)

List 4 (p. 9)

List 5 (p. 10)

List 6 (p. 12)

List 7 (p. 13)

List 9 (p. 15)

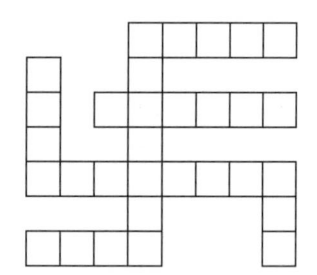

List 10 (p. 16)

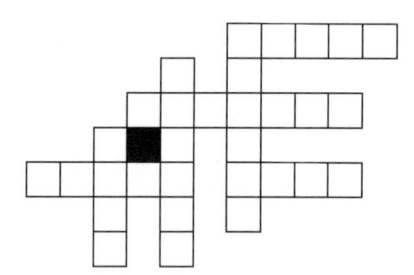

List 11 (p. 18)

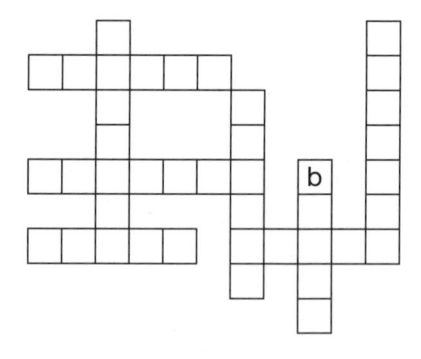

List 12 (p. 19)

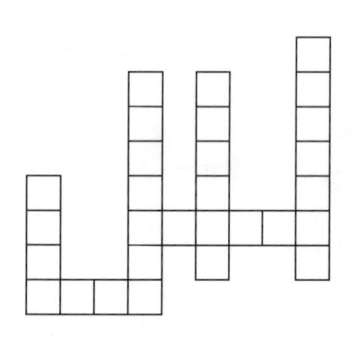

List 14 (p. 21)

List 15 (p. 22)

This page may be photocopied for classroom use.

©Pearson Education New Zealand Limited 2001

List 16 (p. 26)

List 17 (p. 27)

List 19 (p. 29)

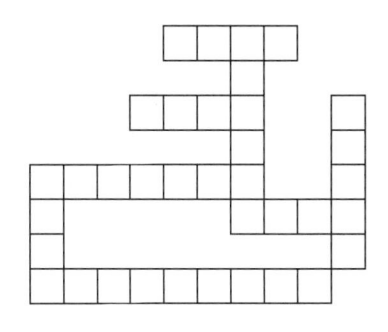

List 20 (p. 30)

List 21 (p. 32)

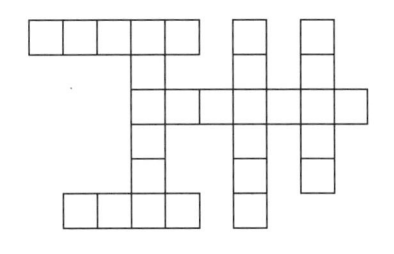

List 22 (p. 33)

List 24 (p. 35)

List 25 (p. 36)

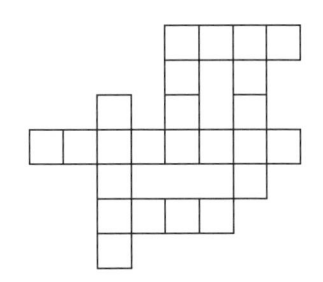

List 26 (p. 38)

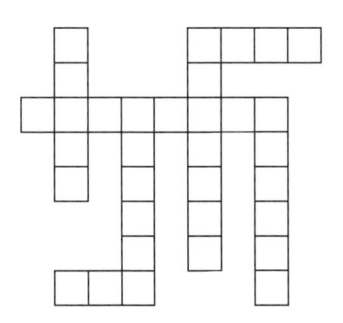

List 27 (p. 39)

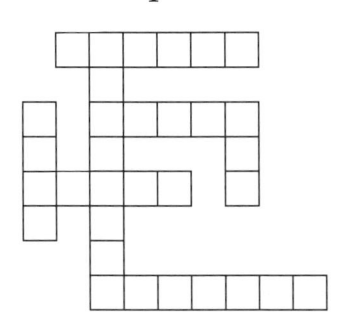

List 29 (p. 41)

List 30 (p. 42)

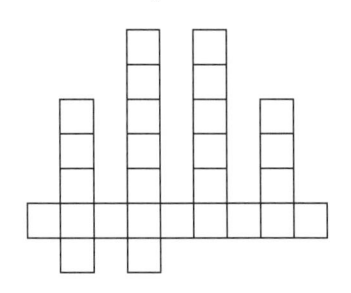

48

List 31 (p. 44)

List 32 (p. 45)

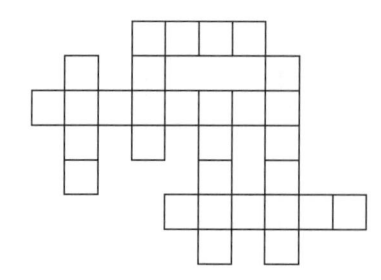

List 34 (p. 47)

List 35 (p. 48)

I hope the children enjoy these puzzles.

I'd like to try some.

Me too!

Puzzle grids
You Can Spell Mastery Set 6

List 2 (p. 7)

List 7 (p. 13)

List 12 (p. 19)

This page may be photocopied for classroom use.

©Pearson Education New Zealand Limited 2001

49

List 17 (p. 27)   List 22 (p. 33)   List 27 (p. 39)

List 32 (p. 45)

I hope the children enjoy these puzzles.

Can I do some?

Photocopying these puzzle grids saves time.

Puzzle grids
You Can Spell Mastery Set 7

List 3 (p. 7)   List 8 (p. 13)

List 13 (p. 19)   List 18 (p. 27)

This page may be photocopied for classroom use.   ©Pearson Education New Zealand Limited 2001

50

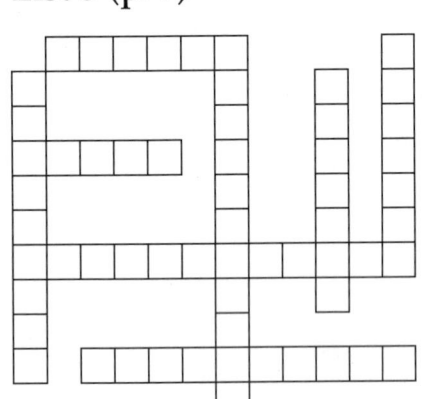

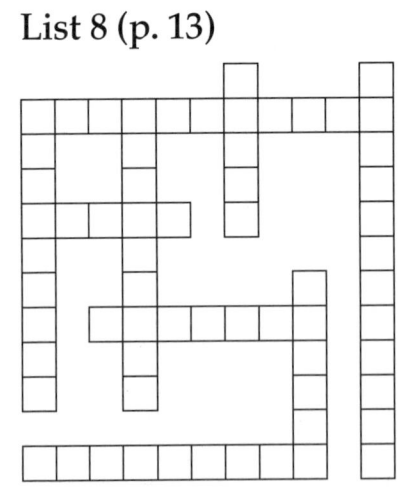

List 23 (p. 33)

List 28 (p. 39)

List 33 (p. 45)

These look like fun.

Are these puzzles hard to do?

No, Jem. The words are all in the spelling lists.

Puzzle grids
You Can Spell Mastery Set 8

List 3 (p. 7)

List 8 (p. 13)

This page may be photocopied for classroom use.

©Pearson Education New Zealand Limited 2001

List 13 (p. 19)

List 18 (p. 27)

List 23 (p. 33)

List 28 (p. 39)

List 33 (p. 45)

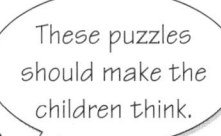

These puzzles should make the children think.

You need some problem-solving skills for them.

There are many books of word puzzles in the shops. You can have lots of fun with them.

This page may be photocopied for classroom use.

©Pearson Education New Zealand Limited 2001

4 Progress graphs (Score sheets)

Name:

Date started:

Diploma date:

Tough Ones from Mastery Set 4

Tough Ones going to Mastery Set 6

You Can Spell

Mastery Set 5

PROGRESS GRAPH

Date																																				
Score																																				

Scores: 16, 15, 14, 13, 12, 11, 10, 9, 8, 7, 6, 5, 4, 3, 2, 1

Lists: 1, 2, 3, 4, 5, 6, 7, 8, 9, 10, 11, 12, 13, 14, 15, 16, 17, 18, 19, 20, 21, 22, 23, 24, 25, 26, 27, 28, 29, 30, 31, 32, 33, 34, 35

Tough Ones

This page may be photocopied for classroom use.

©Pearson Education New Zealand Limited 2001

You Can Spell

Mastery Set ☐

Name:
Date started:
Diploma date:

Tough Ones from Mastery Set ☐

Tough Ones going to Mastery Set ☐

PROGRESS GRAPH

Date																																			
Score																																			

Score rows: 20, 19, 18, 17, 16, 15, 14, 13, 12, 11, 10, 9, 8, 7, 6, 5, 4, 3, 2, 1

Lists: 1, 2, 3, 4, 5, 6, 7, 8, 9, 10, 11, 12, 13, 14, 15, 16, 17, 18, 19, 20, 21, 22, 23, 24, 25, 26, 27, 28, 29, 30, 31, 32, 33, 34, 35

Tough Ones

This page may be photocopied for classroom use.

©Pearson Education New Zealand Limited 2001

5   Diplomas

Spelling Diploma

....

has completed Mastery Set 5 of the *You Can Spell* programme and is now ready for the senior Sets.

Teacher: ....

Date: ....

Principal:..

Spelling Diploma

....

has completed Mastery Set 5 of the *You Can Spell* programme and is now ready for the senior Sets.

Teacher: ....

Date: ....

Principal:..

Spelling Diploma

....

has completed Mastery Set 6 of the
You Can Spell programme and is
now able to spell more than 2300 words.

Teacher: ....

Date: ....

Principal: ....

Spelling Diploma

....

has completed Mastery Set 6 of the
You Can Spell programme and is
now able to spell more than 2300 words.

Teacher: ....

Date: ....

Principal: ....

Spelling Diploma

....

has completed Mastery Set 7 of the *You Can Spell* programme and is now ready for the final Set.

Teacher: ....

Date: ....

Principal: ....

Spelling Diploma

....

has completed Mastery Set 7 of the *You Can Spell* programme and is now ready for the final Set.

Teacher: ....

Date: ....

Principal: ....

Spelling Diploma

....
has completed Mastery Set 8 of the
You Can Spell programme and
is now a confident speller.

Teacher: ....

Date: ....

Principal: ....

Spelling Diploma

....
has completed Mastery Set 8 of the
You Can Spell programme and
is now a confident speller.

Teacher: ....

Date: ....

Principal: ....

This page may be photocopied for classroom use. ©Pearson Education New Zealand Limited 2001

You Can Spell
Centrefold Spelling Project Award

This is to certify that

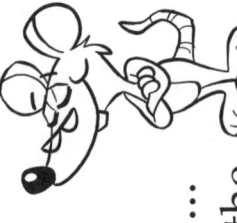

....

has made a good job of completing the centrefold project for Mastery Set ....

Date: ....

Teacher: ....

Principal: ....

This page may be photocopied for classroom use.

©Pearson Education New Zealand Limited 2001

6 School records

You Can Spell
Teacher's workplan record for Mastery Sets 5 to 8

Teacher: .... Room: ....

Group	Group	Group	Group
Set	Set	Set	Set
Names	Names	Names	Names

List	Pretest date	List	Pretest date	List	Pretest date	List	Pretest date
1		1		1		1	
2		2		2		2	
3		3		3		3	
4		4		4		4	
5		5		5		5	
6		6		6		6	
7		7		7		7	
8		8		8		8	
9		9		9		9	
10		10		10		10	
11		11		11		11	
12		12		12		12	
13		13		13		13	
14		14		14		14	
15		15		15		15	
16		16		16		16	
17		17		17		17	
18		18		18		18	
19		19		19		19	
20		20		20		20	
21		21		21		21	
22		22		22		22	
23		23		23		23	
24		24		24		24	
25		25		25		25	
26		26		26		26	
27		27		27		27	
28		28		28		28	
29		29		29		29	
30		30		30		30	

This page may be photocopied for classroom use.   ©Pearson Education New Zealand Limited 2001

ns
You Can Spell

Teacher's workplan – reviews, 'Tough Ones' and dictation

Teacher: .... Room: .... Class: ....

Names

Group 1 Set ☐	Group 2 Set ☐	Group 3 Set ☐	Group 4 Set ☐

Date started _____ _____ _____ _____

Review and Tough Ones

Lists	Date	Lists	Date	Lists	Date	Lists	Date

Dictation

Unit	Date	Unit	Date	Unit	Date	Unit	Date

Teaching Points/ Evaluation

Date ended _____ _____ _____ _____

This page may be photocopied for classroom use.   ©Pearson Education New Zealand Limited 2001

You Can Spell
Pupil Record

School: ....

Name _____ Date of birth _____

Start date Set One _____

or Selection test date _____ Set _____ Score _____ Set _____ Score _____

Set _____ Score _____ Set _____ Score _____

PROGRESS

Date completed

| Set 1 | Set 2 | Set 3 | Set 4 |
| Set 5 | Set 6 | Set 7 | Set 8 |

Date Comment   Date Comment

_____ _____   _____ _____
_____ _____   _____ _____
_____ _____   _____ _____
_____ _____   _____ _____

You Can Spell
Pupil Record

School: ....

Name _____ Date of birth _____

Start date Set One _____

or Selection test date _____ Set _____ Score _____ Set _____ Score _____

Set _____ Score _____ Set _____ Score _____

PROGRESS

Date completed

| Set 1 | Set 2 | Set 3 | Set 4 |
| Set 5 | Set 6 | Set 7 | Set 8 |

Date Comment   Date Comment

_____ _____   _____ _____
_____ _____   _____ _____
_____ _____   _____ _____
_____ _____   _____ _____

This page may be photocopied for classroom use. ©Pearson Education New Zealand Limited 2001

You Can Spell — Transfer Record

Name: _____

Class: _____

School: _____

Last date of attendance: _____

Mastery Set: _____ Last completed list: _____

Signed: _____ (Teacher)

You Can Spell — Transfer Record

Name: _____

Class: _____

School: _____

Last date of attendance: _____

Mastery Set: _____ Last completed list: _____

Signed: _____ (Teacher)

You Can Spell — Transfer Record

Name: _____

Class: _____

School: _____

Last date of attendance: _____

Mastery Set: _____ Last completed list: _____

Signed: _____ (Teacher)

You Can Spell — Transfer Record

Name: _____

Class: _____

School: _____

Last date of attendance: _____

Mastery Set: _____ Last completed list: _____

Signed: _____ (Teacher)

You Can Spell — Transfer Record

Name: _____

Class: _____

School: _____

Last date of attendance: _____

Mastery Set: _____ Last completed list: _____

Signed: _____ (Teacher)

You Can Spell — Transfer Record

Name: _____

Class: _____

School: _____

Last date of attendance: _____

Mastery Set: _____ Last completed list: _____

Signed: _____ (Teacher)

You Can Spell — Transfer Record

Name: _____

Class: _____

School: _____

Last date of attendance: _____

Mastery Set: _____ Last completed list: _____

Signed: _____ (Teacher)

You Can Spell — Transfer Record

Name: _____

Class: _____

School: _____

Last date of attendance: _____

Mastery Set: _____ Last completed list: _____

Signed: _____ (Teacher)

This page may be photocopied for classroom use.

8 Dictation exercises

You Can Spell – Dictation

Mastery Set 5

To follow Unit 1: **Reading the Newspaper**
Reading the newspaper keeps me up to date. I can find out what is on at the museum, what time the churches have services and where to find a good piano teacher. Thousands of people use newspapers for all kinds of reasons. They may want to sell an old van, buy a mower or find out which film is showing on TV. Yes. The newspaper is more than just a means of keeping up with the latest news.

To follow Unit 2: **The Circus**
For a treat in September Nana bought tickets for the circus. When we got there the clown pretended that a dog was chasing him and trying to bite him. He was angry but we only laughed when he tried to shoot the dog with a water pistol. The jet missed the dog and hit the crowd instead. In the final act a woman did a western act with a rope which she used to tie up a horse. Then the clown came in again and he got tied up too.

To follow Unit 3: **The Fly on the Cheese**
The blowfly dropped from the sky diving straight at the block of cheese on the table. I could tell that he had deep and dirty thoughts of stealing my cheese and anything else that I was ready to eat. I took a great swat at him. It was awful. I missed the fly, hit the cheese, knocked over the juice and tipped up the salad. I have no pity for flies.

To follow Unit 4: **Winter**
When I awoke I could tell that the June and July winter season had started. The cold crept through the thin clothing I was wearing. I reached for something warmer then I opened the back door. What a sight. Snow covered the ground in the cold starlight like a great white sheet. I stepped outside, lost my balance on the icy path and fell against the fence post. I hope the jolly snow melts soon.

To follow Unit 5: **The Robber**
My twin sister is quite useful. She's always helpful like the night a robber came to our house. First I heard his steps creeping along the porch. Then I heard him turn the key in the lock. Suddenly he was at our bedroom door and then my sister let out a yell. What a mess. The silly robber raced from the house trying to steal our jewels as he went. The dog's bark frightened him so much that he fell in the swimming pool. It was easy for the police to catch him after that.

To follow Unit 6: **The Pet Parade**
This year there were eighty animals in our school's pet parade. It was a lovely day to be outdoors. I was pleased when my calf won the silver cup for the best trained pet. A goat led the grand parade around the school ground. Suddenly she gave a leap and started to dash towards the crowd. A bee had stung her right on the end of her nose.

To follow Unit 7: **In the Cave**
When the storm began we entered a deep cave with a stream flowing through it. Every person felt upset as lightning struck and we heard the thunder roll above us. As night fell the gale drove the clouds swiftly across the moon. By the light of electric torches we made a meal by heating vegetables and some tinned meat in our only cooking pot. It wasn't much of a feast. Later we slid into our sleeping bags on the hard rocky floor of the cave. Most of us woke several times in the night.

You Can Spell – Dictation

Mastery Set 6

To follow Unit 1: **The Accident**
What an accident! All he did was trip over the brick. Then he fell sideways, crashing into the wooden post before falling down the steps. That wouldn't have been too bad if he hadn't also bitten his tongue and caught his arm in the barbed wire fence. He wasn't very cheerful about being taken to hospital for tripping over a brick.

To follow Unit 2: **Trade**
In New Zealand the cities of Auckland, Wellington, Christchurch and Dunedin rely upon harbours for their trade. In recent times they have exported farm produce and imported manufactured goods. Most of this has been transported by sea. Trade can be a worry for a country with such a small population. We should always try to sell enough to cover what we buy. This is hard to do especially in years when the harvests are poor.

To follow Unit 3: **Technology**
We are all aware of the speed at which technology is advancing. New technical developments are happening all the time. It was not long ago that the computer was a rare thing and videos belonged in TV studios. Now simply by pushing buttons you can open a car door, cook in a microwave oven, use a calculator and even check your spelling. It is amazing that the discovery of electricity could lead to all that in a little over one hundred years.

To follow Unit 4: **Winter Sports**
I really like winter sports so it is easy for me to leave my cosy bed and warm heater to go to the frozen pond set in the snow-clad hills to practise my skating or ski down a snowy slope. I even find the first frost of the season exciting and when the snow comes I am always happy to burn off some energy in a snowball fight with my friends.

To follow Unit 5: **Early Times**
History reminds us of the hard life that people had in ancient times. They depended upon horses and the canoe for transport and had very little machinery to make life easier. Leather and timber were important raw materials that had to be worked by skilful tradesmen. Women wove the family blankets and the hunter's only weapons were his crude knife and his bow and arrow.

To follow Unit 6: **The Wedding**
We're getting ready for Tina's wedding. She is marrying a neighbour of ours. Almost the whole neighbourhood is coming to the celebration, there's no time to spare. I have to set out the furniture and welcome the visitors as they arrive. There will be mountains of food including roast goose and dishes of crab meat. Some guests will make speeches and everyone will drink toasts with wine.

After Unit 7: **Homework Excuses**
I think we are really honest with our excuses about homework. We aren't criminals.
John said, "It's really strange. Suddenly a rocket landed. A robot got out and snatched the homework out of my hand."
I didn't want a bad mark so I said, "It was raining and I thought I might be absent so I left my homework under my pillow so it wouldn't get wet."

You Can Spell – Dictation

Mastery Set 7

To follow Unit 1:
Fur, Feathers and Others
Years ago creatures were labelled as being either fur or feathers. A gorilla would be fur and an eagle feathers. The animal kingdom is not that simple. We would need to add scale or fins to include all the fish and shell to include the oyster. The koala bear might be fur but really deserves a better label while the alligator doesn't fit any of these categories. Fortunately, science has developed a better system of classification. Words like mammal and reptile are much more precise.

To follow Unit 2:
Education
A recent statement by a well-respected professor suggests that if children achieve a good level of primary education they will have an advantage for the rest of their lives. What a nuisance! I was hoping to have fun at school by playing sports, being idle, not wearing out my memory with thoughtful things and probably catching up when I'm older. It's just not fair for this professor to ruin my young life in this way.

To follow Unit 3:
Fibulus the Parrot
There are times when I think that I need protection from my impossibly noisy parrot. Since we became acquainted it has been one unfortunate experience after another. I don't think that I will ever be able to make progress with him. He is always delighted when he messes up the knitting, hides my necklace, rips open envelopes and is rude to religious people. He is such a tease.

To follow Unit 4:
My Ancestors
My ancestors are a mixture but I'm not ashamed of them. They have had a range of occupations. There was a poet and a soldier in uniform that they made a statue of. He was very courageous. Then there was a shopkeeper and a foolish fellow who became a prisoner. I have photographs of the recent ones like my great uncle who worked on the wharves and then I have some photos of unidentified aunts that must have been taken shortly after the camera was invented.

To follow Unit 5:
Fighting Crime
Normally it is the police that fight crime but on rare occasions even they have to call on extra help to restore order. It is scary when you realise that a situation can be so difficult to control that the police need help. One recent overseas example occurred when ordinary people began to quarrel. They became so violent that the safety of others was threatened. It developed into a riot and even intelligent people lost their heads as they began to wreck vehicles, smash windows and start fires. That's when the police asked the military for help.

To follow Unit 6:
Fried Hedgehog
If you look through the word lists for Unit Six you will find some quite amazing ideas. Apart from the fried hedgehog in List Twenty-nine, there is a political recipe and a kangaroo magnet. You will also find dull fairies and a lung mount in List Twenty-eight and with a little effort you could imagine a university widow and a trapped variety zone. It's odd to think of onion planning or trying to sniff subtraction or maybe they are just accidents from the Anyhow Booklet.

To follow Unit 7:
Camping
It is good recreation and it helps to build character when young people set off to explore distant places and camp out at night. Friendships are strengthened as they co-operate to build a bonfire and cook sausages. There is usually a fair bit of amusement when they unpack and find that the torch or kettle has been left behind. They become self-reliant as they make decisions or solve problems together, but most of all they are sharing an exciting and enjoyable experience.

You Can Spell – Dictation

Mastery Set 8

To follow Unit 1:
Antarctica
Scott Base in Antarctica was named after a gallant explorer who perished under canvas with other members of his party while trying to make a return journey to the South Pole. Even today with modern equipment and technology this land is not to be treated carelessly. Any journey that is undertaken requires good management, precise navigation and an assurance of adequate accommodation. Of course there is one creature that doesn't need to take any of these precautions in Antarctica. That's the penguin.

After Unit 2:
The Encyclopedia
My young son has complained that spelling 'encyclopedia' is bad enough but trying to read one is impossible. He really is an emergency about to turn into a catastrophe. Why can't he understand that it is a massive catalogue of knowledge, a reservoir of marvellous descriptions and not some frightening volume designed to bring perspiration to the brow of our desperate little genius. He maintains that the encyclopedia is only useful as a weight to put on top of something you are trying to glue.

To follow Unit 3:
The Centennial
We held the celebration of our school's centennial last weekend. It was unforgettable. An enormous crowd attended, filled with enthusiasm for the occasion. Prominent people made speeches at the banquet but the best event for me was picnicking in the school gardens. It was there that I appreciated the opportunity to renew my acquaintance with many of my old school chums and enquire about their lives and families. The grounds had been beautifully prepared for the occasion.

To follow Unit 4:
Gymnastics
"Welcome to the National Championships," said the official. "We shall begin with the Certificate Events." It all sounded so formal. My confidence waned and I was sure that I was heading for disaster. I had to overcome my nervousness. The vast gymnasium fell silent as I advanced to the mat. Suddenly the lights came on and the music started. I danced and bounced through the somersaults of my routine. Nothing could interrupt my concentration. It only seemed like a few seconds and then it was over. The judges' cards were raised: 10-9-10-9-10.

To follow Unit 5:
In the Laboratory
Professor Jade was brilliant. In her laboratory she had perfected a new power unit for the submarine and the helicopter. Now she was optimistic that she possessed the ability to use a similar device to power a spaceship. I assisted her to assemble those massive cylinders and I marvelled over the precision of her organisation. Jade needed no chemistry for this device. When she finally launched it the ship burst through the heavens towards the moon. The humble rubber band had triumphed once again in humankind's endeavour to conquer space.

To follow Unit 6:
Athletics
Henry is weird but he is practical. He knew that he would get two points just for entering in each event in our athletic sports, the teachers call it encouragement. Henry entered the lot. He came last in all the races, threw the discus into the astonished crowd of spectators, dropped the shotput on an official's toe and made a real exhibition of himself in the jumps. When this hero stepped up to hurl the javelin we all tried to run away. For once he got it right. It sailed through the air and he won the event with a new school record. Not only that, he had so many points he became our athletics champion!

To follow Unit 7:
The Earthquake
It took us by surprise. Earthquakes always do. One moment I was saying, "Have another sandwich," the next the table, the chairs, everything went rocking like a roller coaster. Cabinets tumbled over. Anything moveable moved. Delicate things crumbled and the ceiling sagged. I watched helplessly as my favourite ornaments tumbled off the dresser shelves. It was a nightmare. Just as quickly as it had begun it stopped. We stared at each other. Outside we could hear people shrieking. It was awful.